NATIVE AMERICAN WRITERS

MULTICULTURAL VOICES

MULTICULTURAL VOICES

NATIVE AMERICAN WRITERS

STEVEN OTFINOSKI

CHELSEA HOUSE
PUBLISHERS
An imprint of Infobase Publishing

MULTICULTURAL VOICES: Native American Writers

Copyright © 2010 by Infobase Publishing

Chelsea House
An imprint of Infobase Publishing
132 West 31st Street
New York NY 10001

Library of Congress Cataloging-in-Publication Data
Otfinoski, Steven.
   Native American writers / Steven Otfinoski.
      p. cm.—(Multicultural voices)
Includes bibliographical references and index.
ISBN 978-1-60413-314-1 (hardcover)
   1. American literature—Indian authors—History and criticism—Juvenile literature.
2. American literature—Indian authors—Stories, plots, etc—Juvenile literature.
3. American literature—Indian authors—Themes, motives—Juvenile literature.
4. Indian authors—United States—Biography—Juvenile literature. 5. Indians in literature—Juvenile literature. I. Title. II. Series.
   PS153.I52O72 2010
   810.9'897—dc22   2009041334

Chelsea House books are available at special discounts when purchased in bulk quantities for businesses, associations, institutions, or sales promotions. Please call our Special Sales Department in New York at (212) 967-8800 or (800) 322-8755.

You can find Chelsea House on the World Wide Web at
http://www.chelseahouse.com

Series design by Lina Farinella
Composition by IBT Global, Inc., Troy NY
Cover printed by IBT Global, Inc., Troy NY
Book printed and bound by IBT Global, Inc., Troy NY
Date printed: February 2010
Printed in the United States of America

10 9 8 7 6 5 4 3 2 1

This book is printed on acid-free paper.

All links and Web addresses were checked and verified to be correct at the time of publication. Because of the dynamic nature of the Web, some addresses and links may have changed since publication and may no longer be valid.

CONTENTS

OVERVIEW

"I GREW UP IN TWO WORLDS and straddle between both worlds even now," N. Scott Momaday, known as the dean of Native American writers, has said. This statement could summarize the experience of many Native Americans in the twenty-first century and forms the focus of much of contemporary Native American literature's thematic concerns.

Native American life and culture were permanently altered by the gradual dispossession of ancestral lands by white settlers, a process that began soon after the first Europeans landed in present-day Virginia and Massachusetts. Gradually pushed farther and farther west, the native inhabitants made their last stand on the Great Plains and in the deserts of the Southwest. The systematic destruction of Native American society and culture by the U.S. government is an often-told story and a stark reminder of the violation, violence, and cruelty that have marked certain chapters of American history. Restricted to federal reservations where there were few opportunities to find meaningful employment and cut off from the traditions and mores of their ancestors, many modern-day Indians continue to live in abject poverty, their only solace found all too often in self-destructive or addictive behaviors.

The struggle to reconnect with the rich heritage of the past—its folkways, values, and traditions—is a common theme in the work of many of the writers who followed in Momaday's wake. The search for identity in a white-dominated world preoccupies and drives these writers, whether they be Kiowa (Momaday), Laguna Pueblo (Leslie Marmon Silko), or Oglala (Louise Erdrich).

Native American writers have not only drawn on the rich traditions of their native literature, the myths, legends, and folk tales—they have incorporated the varying styles and structures of native storytelling into their own novels and stories. A traditionally chronological narrative is commonly forsaken for a circular narrative structure that folds back on itself. Time may be fluid, plots nonlinear,

7

with events occurring out of sequence, forming a pattern of intent that is often only understood at a work's conclusion. The line dividing reality from the fantastical is also often crossed; dreams, visions, and ghosts play as major a role in the plots as the living, human characters. These elements are just a few of the common threads unifying the Native American literary tradition, which has become as diverse as its practitioners.

Modern Native American literature arguably began with the publication in 1968 of N. Scott Momaday's novel *House Made of Dawn*, which incorporated many of the features of traditional native storytelling. When the novel received the Pulitzer Prize for Fiction the following year, the award and the subsequent recognition it brought helped put the critical stamp of approval on Native American literature and paved the way for a group of gifted writers to emerge and add their voices to a growing body of work and the burgeoning artistic movement often referred to as the Native American renaissance.

A tradition of Native American literature existed before Momaday's arrival, but it was not until the 1960s that Native American writers had found a way to tell stories derived from the rich indigenous history that stretched back to pre-Columbian days. Absorbing other influences, Native American authors also started looking to European models in their writing. Works about Native Americans published from the 1700s onward were mainly ethnographies, biographies, or histories written mainly by non-natives and so-called "faux Indians" whose true heritage was often questioned or suspect. This search for native authenticity continues today. Such esteemed writers as the late Michael Dorris, for instance, have been accused of not actually being Native American.

The first known novel written by a Native American is *The Life and Adventures of Joaquin Murieta: The Celebrated California Bandit,* published in 1854 by John Rollin Ridge, who was part Cherokee. This fictional version of the real-life Murieta's exploits is known for its sharp critique of racism mainly as expressed toward Mexican Americans, not Native Americans. In his later life, Ridge worked as a newspaper editor in California and was a strong advocate of American Indians assimilating into white society.

John Miller Oskison, also Cherokee, was another influential magazine editor whose short story "Only the Master Shall Praise" won a *Century* magazine prize in 1899. Osage Indian John Joseph Matthews's first book, *Wa'kan-tah: The Osage and the White Man's Road*, was a best-seller in 1929 and was named a Book-of-the-Month Club selection. His only novel, *Sundown* (1934), was the semiautobiographical story of a young Osage who retuned to his native community after college and military service to find himself alienated and alone. This same theme and plot would surface again in such later Native American novels as Momaday's *House Made of Dawn* and Leslie Marmon Silko's *Ceremony*.

Mourning Dove, a pseudonym for the woman author Hum-isha-me (English name Christal Quintasket) published *Cogewea the Half-Blood: A Depiction of the*

CARTER CURTIS REVARD

Biography

A HIGHLY RESPECTED WRITER whose work reflects his Native American heritage, Carter Curtis Revard has lived a double life as a poet and a scholar who specializes in medieval literature.

He was born, along with his twin sister, on March 25, 1931, in Pawhuska, Oklahoma, an Osage Indian Agency town. His father, McGuire Revard, left the family when Carter was very young. His mother, Thelma Louise Camp, married another Osage, Addison Jump, and they had four more children. Carter attended a one-room reservation schoolhouse through eighth grade in Buck Creek Valley, Oklahoma, where his family later moved. Many of his poems deal with his childhood experiences at Buck Creek. With his twin sister, Maxine, Carter was the school janitor. As a young man, he worked harvesting hay and training greyhounds to race. He attended Bartlesville College High School and won a radio quiz scholarship to the University of Tulsa.

After earning a bachelor of arts (B.A.) degree in 1952 at Tulsa, Revard earned a second B.A. at Oxford University in England, which he attended on a Rhodes Scholarship. He earned his Ph.D. degree from Yale University in 1959. Revard taught literature at Amherst College in Massachusetts from 1956 to 1961 and then joined the faculty at Washington University in Saint Louis, Missouri, in 1961. He remained there for more than three decades, retiring in 1997. An expert and leading authority on medieval English literary manuscripts, Revard has written scholarly works on linguistics and Native American literature.

Revard published his first volume of poetry, *Ponca War Dancers*, in 1980. *Cowboys and Indians Christmas Shopping* appeared in 1992, and *An Eagle Nation*, his best-known poetry collection, was published in 1997. The following year he published a memoir about his childhood and family ancestry, *Family*

13

Matters, Tribal Affairs. His most recent poems are collected in *How the Songs Came Down* (2005).

In 2005, Revard received the Lifetime Achievement Award from Native Writers' Circle of the Americas. He was the recipient of the American Indian Festival of Words Author Award in 2007. For many years, he served on the board of the American Indian Center of Saint Louis. Revard's wife, Stella, is a scholar and expert on the English poet John Milton. The couple has four children.

Much of Revard's poetry is written in conversational English and is autobiographical in nature. He often weaves allegorical stories from Native American folklore into his poetry, some of which is cast in the style or form of traditional English verse. Revard's poetry reflects a deep love of and wonder about the natural world; a skepticism of authority, especially politicians; a buoyant sense of humor; and a strong connection to the myths, legends, and traditions of his people. "How time dawned on mind and was beaded into language amazes me the way an orb-spider's web or computer-chip does," he wrote in the introduction to *An Eagle Nation.*

Ponca War Dances
Summary and Analysis

Revard's first collection of poetry supports Norma C. Wilson's assessment that "[n]o other Native poet has been able to so fully articulate in English words the relationship between ancient tribal myths and modern life."

In poem after poem, Revard contrasts the richness of the mythic Indian past with the confusing, often questionable present. In "People of the Stars," he refers to the creation story that the Wazhazhe (the native name for the Osage nation) came from the stars and after they die will return there. He reflects on this as he descends literally from the sky on a plane to the glittering lights of Las Vegas, the nation's gambling capital. There he will "Shoot craps at the Stardust Inn / and talk of Indians and their Trickster Tales." The juxtaposition of the gaming tables and the eternal stars makes for an ironic comment about contemporary native life, which is supported and sustained in many tribal organizations by gambling.

In other poems, Revard contrasts the past with a more personal family history. "Wazhazhe Grandmother" describes a visit to his grandparents' ancestral home at Bird Creek when he was six years old and recounts the rich heritage of the tribe in that place.

The book's title poem, one of the longest in the collection, is a tribute and celebration of his Uncle Gus McDonald, "the greatest of Ponca dancers." A colorful character, Gus shows his respect for the traditional ways of his people not just in his dancing. In the poem's first section, Gus confounds his nephew Buck's new wife by not talking to her directly during a visit. She mistakes this age-honored form of Ponca respect for women as a sign that he does not like her.

In the second section, the poem's narrator, Mike (Revard's Irish nickname), sees Gus dance for the first time and is amazed by his agility:

Potbellied but quick-footed went
Twirling and drifting
Stomping with the hawkwing a-hover then
                                    Leaping

Spinning light as
A leaf in a whirlwind.

In the third section, Mike and his Indian friends are driving to a memorial feast in the late Gus's honor in 1974 at an auditorium in Ponca City, Oklahoma. The time is critical, because it is a period of high tension between Native American activists who belong to the American Indian Movement (AIM) and governmental authorities. The young people's car is followed by a state police cruiser, but they arrive at the feast without incident. Later, one of Mike's cousins, Carter Camp, is arrested for disarming a postal inspector at Wounded Knee, South Dakota, the previous year and is sentenced to three years in prison. He accepts his fate because he is "back among my people now."

In the fourth section of the poem, we are told that Gus's niece Serena has named her Indian crafts shop Shongeh-Ska, Gus's Indian name, meaning "white horse." The appropriation for commercial purposes of Gus's spirit and the heritage of the past are less important to the poet, however, than the memory of Gus and his dancing.

For those who saw him dance,
        And learned from him the way,
            He is dancing still.
Come to White Eagle in the summer time,
            Indians dance in summer time—
He is back with his people now.

While "Ponca War Dancers" is not without its ironies, other poems are savagely satirical, perhaps none more so than "Discovery of the New World." Here, Revard imagines the discovery of the Americas by Christopher Columbus in reverse. The discoverers are little green men from outer space who take over the earth. White people feel what it was like to be colonized, exploited, and obliterated by more powerful beings. Like the explorers and settlers of the New World, these aliens are ruthless in their handling of the natives.

We need their space and oxygen
Which they do not know how to use,

Yet they will not give up their gas unforced,
And we feel sure,
Whatever our "agreements" made this morning,
We'll have to cook them all:
The more we cook this orbit,
The fewer next time around.

Major Themes

"Revard's poetry portrays American Indians not as culturally isolated victims resisting pressures from the outside, but as agents of global history," writes Ellen L. Arnold in her introduction to *The Salt Companion to Carter Revard*. Perhaps the most impressive of these agents are the Osage and Ponca people who are celebrated in many of the poems. The connection of past to present in Indian life is a major theme running through Revard's collection. Other central thematic concerns are the dispossession of the native lands through the centuries and the power of memory to re-create the past and provide a guide for the future.

Loss of Native American Lands

In "Wazhazhe Grandmother," Revard chronicles the history of the Osages as the U.S. government moves them from Missouri to Kansas and then to Indian Territory; the region would later become the state of Oklahoma. The Osages, he explains, are the only nation in Indian Territory to keep ownership of the subsurface minerals contained in their tribal lands. Their relative security, however, does not protect them from the rampant greed of white developers. Revard's grandparents' land is submerged with water to provide recreation and help create tourist-related businesses for outsiders. Once again, the family must leave its home and move to the city of Pawhuska. The land that Revard conjures in other poems, as he remembers it in his childhood, is gone. All that remain are his memories as set down in his poems.

An Eagle Nation

Summary and Analysis

Carter Revard calls *An Eagle Nation*, his third collection of poetry, "a giveaway special." What he is giving away are a wealth of poems that are suffused with a lifetime of living, study, and love. A writer who has spent most of his professional life in the halls of academia could be expected to write poetry that is esoteric and complex. Yet the poetry and prose pieces that are interspersed in Revard's collection are surprisingly accessible—colloquial, conversational, and straightforward. For all his years as a university teacher and scholar, he has lost none of the sense of wonder of his childhood growing up near Buck Creek, Oklahoma, a magical locale he returns to time and again in his poetry. Yet he also writes about the world of literature and nature, and the wonders of natural science that come vibrantly alive in his poems.

An Eagle Nation is divided into three sections. The first, "An Eagle Nation," deals in large part with childhood memories, Native American lore, and contemporary Indian life. The world has changed since his childhood, and Revard feels it is not necessarily a change for the better. In "Rock Shelter," he contrasts the glorious landscape of his youth with the world today, where asphalt and wire fences replace the rocks of Buck Creek. Everything is up for sale, even the cosmos itself:

> *Galaxies, before long, may*
> *Be sold for profit, once the first space ship has*
> *Claimed one and the next has*
> *Come to kill all those before.*

In "Where to Hang Them," the poet turns a critical eye to the politicians who have shaped this new world. The poem ends with this terse couplet:

> *The place to hang our rulers' portraits*
> *Is on post office walls.*

Revard is referring here to the wanted posters of criminals that were traditionally displayed in post offices.

The poet's anger toward society is leavened with a sense of humor that can be refreshingly self-deprecating. In "Parading with the V.F.W. (Veterans of Foreign Wars)," he recalls marching in Saint Louis with other Indians in traditional dress. He becomes dismayed when he spots a group of Civil War reenactors wearing the insignia of Custer's Seventh Cavalry. Later, these "authentic" Indians feast on fast food chicken "given the temporary absence of buffalo here in the Gateway to the West, St. Louis."

In the title poem, Revard recalls taking his beloved Aunt Jewell, confined to a wheelchair, to the Oklahoma City Zoo. They see a caged and crippled eagle that will never fly again. The eagle, eyes closed, is unresponsive to all visitors until Aunt Jewell speaks to it in her native Ponca language. Revard does not understand much of what she is saying, but the eagle, which suddenly becomes alert, seems to comprehend her words.

> *She talked a little more, apologizing*
> > *For all of us, I think.*
> *She put one hand up to her eyes and closed them for a while*
> > *Till Casey handed her a handkerchief,*
> > *And she wiped her eyes.*

The old lady's spirits revive when they take her to a huge powwow where her grandson is among the 1,400 dancers performing. The event brings back memories to Jewell of meeting her first husband at a dance years earlier. For Revard, images are conjured of soaring eagles watching the pioneers' wagons crossing the prairie, changing the native people's world forever. The spirit of the people, though, as represented by the eagle, will never die. "We the people . . ." he writes, "are an EAGLE NATION now."

In the second section, "Homework at Oxford," the poems are largely about the poet's travels to England, the Isle of Skye, Yellowstone National Park, and California. No matter how far he roams from Saint Louis, however, Revard often finds things in nature that remind him of his youth in Buck Creek. In the title poem, he stays up all night reading at Oxford University in England and walks across the campus at dawn. The smell of a nearby pasture reminds him of his childhood back in Oklahoma. Many of the landscapes he obverses and describes so richly are near the sea—the rocky Atlantic coast, the coast of the Isle of Skye, the Pacific Palisades north of Santa Monica, California. The sea with its teeming life and birds swirling overhead holds a special fascination for him. Even back home, in the poem "Outside in St. Louis," he see birds that hear the faraway ocean in the city's endless noise.

"Sea-Change," the last section of the book, delves deeply into natural science and the evolving of nature over centuries and millennia. One of the most striking pieces in this part is "Geode," a poem that appeared in a different form in his previous collection, *Cowboys and Indians Christmas Shopping*. The poem opens with a detailed encyclopedic definition of a geode, "a hollow mineral sphere sometimes found in limestone cave systems." In a daring leap of imagination, Revard imagines the stone's formation over eons from the perspective of the geode itself. "I felt / purple quartz-crystals blossom where / my pale flesh had been." For Norma C. Wilson, the poem "demonstrates the poet's capacity to create something of substance and meaning with words. The poem invests with consciousness a feature of nature that white culture considers dead matter." For Revard, with his native sensibility, the geode is alive. In a wry reversal of Jesus's emblematic significance in the Bible, instead of the Word becoming flesh, it becomes stone.

In the title poem of this section, nature's wonders are reduced to a television screen, on which the narrator is watching a program about dolphins and humans. The divers are luring the dolphins with sounds to learn their secret language. Music, while great, can also be used to enslave and harm, as Wagner's music was used by the German Nazis as a soundtrack for Hitler's "master race." Technology can use nature to its own purposes, so this is one sea change that the poet does not trust.

Major Themes

Revard's curiosity about the world of nature and learning infuses his poetry and prose pieces with fascinating images, intriguing juxtapositions, and brilliant parallels. He sees the history and traditions of his own people echoed in that of other peoples and civilizations, a unique perspective built on his vast learning and reading. In *An Eagle Nation*, Revard celebrates his connection with friends, ancestors, and the inhabitants of the natural world. His poems evoke themes of community between humans and the world around them, the importance of the past, and the destructive power of nations and governments.

The Supremacy of Nature

Like many Native Americans past and present, Carter Revard views the natural world as something deeply spiritual and sacred. He is able to find the beauty of nature not just in mountains, eagles, and sunsets but also in rocks, fossils, and the digestive system of a bird. He examines and observes nature in his poetry with the careful studiousness of a biologist but always points out the transcendent element of earthly things.

In the animal world, he especially admires birds, and they appear in many of the poems in this collection, from the caged eagle of "An Eagle Nation" to the cardinal he has a conversation with while the president's plane flies overhead in the prose piece "A Cardinal, New Snow, and Some Firewood."

As Norma C. Wilson points out in her essay on Revard in *The Nature of Native American Poetry,* he opposes the idea put forth by American poet Wallace Stevens that art should be held above nature. For Revard, as for his native ancestors, the natural world, in and of itself, is more awesome and inspiring that anything the intellect of humans can devise.

In "Snowflakes, Waterdrops, Time, Eternity, and So On," one of the last poems in *An Eagle Nation*, Revard praises the unity of nature, explaining that while every snowflake may be unique, "they melt to waterdrops identified / each one with every other." The poem ends with the poet urging us to drink water like "sparkling champagne:"

> *its snowy bubbles briskly*
> *dancing upon our tongues. . . .*
> *within our heads,*
> *but not with grief,*
> *not with regret, only*
> *the knowledge that we'll have*
> *our differences, and may*
> *we thank God for them every day.*

The Distrust of Governments and Authority

For Revard, if nature is to be celebrated, then governments are to be scorned. The modern political state is not the savior of people but often their enemy, Revard believes. In "A Response To Terrorists," he observes the constant struggle between rival nations and poses the question:

Isn't there some way we might
   Get out from under without finding ourselves
   On top and smothering others?

While Native Americans may be all but powerless in this power-mad world, Revard would prefer "our kind of small endangered cultures where the sense of nearly every one of us, . . . / is borne in on us by our smallness, / our clear fragility."

While the world's leaders may look distinguished and speak of peace, they "murder with their tongues, send / surrogates to knife, garrote, beat, poison, torture."

In the poem "Foetal Research," Revard savagely satirizes modern governmental genetic engineering where "a chimp's egg had been fertilized by Superman." It produces twins who voted Republican and Democrat in the next primary.

In the prose piece "The Man Lee Harvey Oswald Missed," Revard notes a not so subtle comparison of Hitler's Germany with our own modern industrial state. Only by recognizing the insanity of the world's governments, he seems to be saying, can we maintain our own sanity and survive.

N. SCOTT MOMADAY

Biography

KNOWN AS "the dean of Native American writers," N. Scott Momaday is the first Native American writer to win a Pulitzer Prize. He was born Navarre Scott Momaday on February 27, 1934, on the Kiowa Reservation in Lawton, Oklahoma. His mother was a writer and his father a painter. They earned their living, however, teaching school on an Indian reservation.

When Scott was one year old, the family moved to Arizona, where he was exposed to the culture of several southwestern tribes, including the Navajo, Apache, and Pueblo. Later, the family moved to New Mexico, where his parents taught for 25 years in an Indian day school at the Jemez Pueblo.

Interested in literature from an early age, Momaday attended the University of New Mexico, where he earned a B.A. in 1958. He then earned a master's degree (1960) and a Ph.D. (1963) from Stanford University in California. Soon after, he began a long and distinguished academic career. Since 1970, Momaday has taught literature at the University of Arizona in Tucson. He is an authority on the poetry of Emily Dickinson and the lesser-known poet Frederick Goddard Tuckerman, whose collected works he has edited. Since 1969, Momaday has also taught a yearly course on Native American oral tradition.

Momaday's first book, *The Journey of Tai-me*, was published in 1967. He later revised it as the multigenre book, *The Way to Rainy Mountain* (1969). His first novel, *House Made of Dawn*, appeared in 1968 and was awarded a Pulitzer Prize the following year. It quickly became identified as a significant breakthrough in bringing Native American literature to the mainstream. Since then, Momaday has written a wide range of works including a memoir (*The Names: A Memoir*, 1976), poetry (*The Gourd Dancer*, 1976), a play (*The Indolent Boys*, 1993), another novel (*The Ancient Child*, 1990), nonfiction (*The Native Americans, Indian Coun-*

try, 1993), and a children's book *(Circle of Wonder: A Native American Christmas Story,* 1994). His most recent work, *In the Bear's House* (1999), is a collection of poems and dialogues.

Momaday has received twelve honorary degrees from various universities, including Yale University, and was the first professor to teach American literature at the University of Moscow. In 2007, he was awarded a National Medal of Arts by President George W. Bush.

Momaday has also narrated documentaries on the West for the Public Broadcasting Service (PBS). Since the 1970s, he has also been a painter and printmaker. A retrospective of his art was exhibited in 1992–93 at Santa Fe's Wheelwright Museum.

Momaday's writing is dense and can be difficult until one comes to understand the complex storytelling techniques he employs. Like other Native American writers, he is concerned with evoking forgotten traditions and rituals to discover personal identity. Memory and the past loom large in nearly all his works, whether fiction, nonfiction, or poetry. Unlike some of his contemporaries, including Carter Curtis Revard and younger writers such as Leslie Marmon Silko and Sherman Alexie, Momaday has little interest in politics or social activism.

House Made of Dawn
Summary and Analysis

N. Scott Momaday's first and most celebrated novel is the story of Abel, a young Pueblo Indian, who returns home from service abroad in World War II alienated and deeply troubled. The novel covers seven years in Abel's life and is told mostly in long flashbacks and in a complicated narrative style that Momaday says was influenced by traditional Kiowa storytelling.

In a prologue, Abel is running in the winter race, a ceremonial footrace that begins the year in his pueblo. As he runs, he looks back on the events of his life, which will comprise most of the rest of the novel. The act of running, portrayed in the novel's opening and conclusion, will become a central metaphor in the narrative.

"The Longhair," the first of the four main sections that the novel is divided into, takes place over seven days in July and August 1945. Abel returns home from his wartime service to the Jemez Pueblo in New Mexico, which the Indians who reside there call Walatona. Momaday first introduces the reader to the landscape, not the humans, in his story. The landscape is a major character in the novel, and Abel's relationship to it serves as the crux of the story. As Robert M. Nelson points out in his study *Place and Vision: The Function of Landscape in Native American Fiction,* Momaday believes the natural landscape to be more important that the limited lives of the characters that tread on it. To stress this, "the narrative component of Part 1 takes form in the past tense, while the component dealing with the landscape is put in the present tense."

On his return, Abel admires the landscape of his home and derives a degree of calm and peace from it. Nevertheless, his view of the landscape is that of the soaring eagle he sights in the sky, the bird looking down on the land with a detached eye. He is not part of the landscape and feels as alienated from it as he is from other people.

The most important person in Abel's life is his grandfather Francisco, his only remaining close relative. Francisco represents the wisdom of the people and the critical link with the past. He was once a ceremonial runner himself and remains a fully integrated member of the pueblo community.

Another stranger who arrives in the area is the well-to-do wife of a Los Angeles doctor, the beautiful Angela Grace St. John. She is staying in neighboring Los Ojos for the medicinal mineral baths. Angela asks Father Olguin, the mission priest, to find someone to cut firewood for the kitchen oven in the old Benevides house where she is staying, the house of the title. Father Olguin sends Abel, and St. John watches, fascinated, as he chops the wood with a relentless intensity. Like Abel, St. John appears to have been wounded by life and is searching for meaning.

The pueblo celebrates the Feast of Santiago with a ritual contest called a rooster pull. Horsemen attempt to pull a white rooster, buried up to its neck, out of the ground. Abel tries to become part of the community by participating in the contest but fails miserably. The winner of this grisly game is Juan Reyes, an albino Indian of mixed heritage. Reyes represents evil and is even described in terms of a serpent. He beats Abel, one of the losers, over the head with the bloodied bird, securing Abel's hatred of him.

When Abel returns to finish chopping the wood for St. John, she seduces him and they have a single sexual encounter. Afterwards, Abel leaves passively, seemingly untouched by the woman's passion. Later, he confronts Juan Reyes in a bar, and the two men go outside to settle their differences. They draw knives, and Abel kills Reyes with the same cold deliberateness with which he earlier chopped the firewood.

The next part of the novel, "The Priest of the Sun," takes place in Los Angeles seven years later, in 1952. After serving six years in prison for the killing of Reyes, Abel has been sent to the city through the government's relocation program. The change of scenery does not offer redemption for Abel, though. He is lying helpless on a beach, recuperating from a severe beating by Martinez, a sadistic Mexican police officer. As he lies there, he has a vision of the footrace that is symbolic and suggestive of his psychic healing. "His skin crawled with excitement," Momaday writes, "he was overcome with longing and loneliness, for suddenly he saw the crucial sense in their going, of old men in white leggings running after evil in the night. They were whole and indispensable in what they did; everything in creation referred to them." Before Abel can join the old men in the race, though, he must look back and reflect on the painful events of the past several years. He recalls a sermon delivered by the Reverend J.B.B. Tosamah, pastor of the Holiness Pan-Indian Rescue Mission and self-proclaimed priest of the sun. Tosamah reinterprets the Scriptures from a Native American perspective and offers a kind of salvation to his followers through the sacred hallucinatory drug peyote.

Abel then recalls his trial for homicide in the death of Juan Reyes. He shows no remorse and offers no defense for what he sees as a ritual act against evil. "They must know that he would kill the white man again, if he had the chance, that there could be no hesitation whatsoever," Abel reasons. "For he would know what the white man was, he would kill him if he could."

Several soldiers who served with Abel during the war testify at the trial to both his courage and seeming imprudent sense of daring as he singlehandedly faced a German tank, dodging bullets while performing a war dance. Convicted and serving his sentence in prison, Abel meets the Indian woman Milly, whose losses are perhaps even greater than his. Her husband died in the war, and she later lost her only child to illness. After his release, Abel and Milly become lovers, but except for her love, his life remains aimless.

The third section, "The Night Chanter," also takes place in 1952. It is narrated by Ben Benally, another Indian who is Abel's roommate, a co-worker at a factory, and a close friend. Along with Milly, Benally tries to help Abel adjust to life after his time in prison but makes little progress. "You could see that he wasn't going to get along around here . . ." Benally says of Abel, "You know, you have to change. That's the only way you can live in a place like this. You have to forget about the way it was, how you grew up and all. Sometimes it's hard, but you have to do it. Well, he didn't want to change, I guess, or he didn't know how."

After Abel is beaten by Martinez and ends up in the hospital, Benally finds Angela St. John and brings her to visit him. Once recuperated, Abel decides to return home to Walatowa by train.

In the last section, "The Dawn Runner," Abel is back at the pueblo, caring for his grandfather who is ill and dying. Francisco tells his grandson about his life as a young warrior, especially the time he killed a bear as a rite of passage. His stories reconnect Abel with his tribal past and give him a direction he lacked before. When he awakens the following morning, Abel finds his grandfather has died during the night. Abel prepares the body for ritual burial and then goes to see Father Olguin and tells him to bury the old man according to pueblo tradition. Then Abel covers his body with ashes and joins the other men in their ritual run into the dawn. As Abel runs, he sings a tribal song. He is in harmony with nature, his people, and himself.

Major Themes

Explaining why the Pulitzer Prize jury chose *House Made of Dawn* for its fiction award in 1969, one jury member cited its "eloquence and intensity of feeling, its freshness of vision and subject, its immediacy of theme."

Many of the themes that run through the novel carry over into Momaday's later work. They include the conflict between Native American and non-native cultures, the sacredness of the land, creation and rebirth, and the strong bond of native people with their heritage and community.

Conflict of Cultures

Momaday has called this theme one of the "central concerns" of his writing. While Abel, the protagonist of his novel, is torn between the values and traditions of his people and those of contemporary white society, he, in many ways, feels a part of neither culture.

Abel grew up in pueblo society and participated in the life of the community, but he never felt fully at home there. He never knew his father, and his mother and brother die when he is still young. The only close relative he has is his grandfather Francisco, whom he fails to connect with in a meaningful way until the last section of the novel.

Characteristically, Abel is drunk on his return, finding alcohol provides the only way for him to cope with his internal conflicts. In the two weeks he spends with his grandfather, he tries to forget the terrible events of the war and reconnect with his past, but his efforts are futile. His experiences in the war, which are related later in the book and through the eyes of other soldiers who served with him, have numbed him to life and its promise. He has a sexual encounter with the sympathetic white woman Angela St. John but feels no intimate connection with her and does not see her again until his friend Benally brings her to his hospital room years later. His attempt to participate in the ceremonial game the rooster pull is a failure, and he is later humiliated by the albino Juan Reyes, who wins the contest and beats him with the bloody bird.

Later, Abel kills Reyes, who he views as an evil force, a witch, with a cold, calculating deliberateness. "It is possible that Abel recognizes himself in the figure of the albino, a mixture of Indian and white," observes Matthias Schubnell in his study of the author and his works. "The killing of the albino is a symbolic representation of the cultural conflict which Abel is trying to resolve."

Creation and Rebirth

The themes of creation and rebirth are central to many Native American myths. In the second section of the novel, Abel's rebirth to life and wholeness begins, ironically, when he is at his lowest point. Having served his term in prison for the death of Reyes, he is beaten savagely by the police officer Martinez and left on a beach, hovering between life and death. The nearby water and the moon overhead are symbols of Abel's rebirth.

This slow process leads Abel from the chaos and confusion of Los Angeles, where he is unable to start a new life for himself, back to the pueblo, where he is reunited with his grandfather. As he lies dying, Francisco tells Abel the stories of the past, bringing the grandson back to an awareness and understanding of his ancestors. In Francisco's death, Abel is reborn, taking on the role of the medicine man and preparing his grandfather for his ritual funeral and burial. The coming dawn is the most potent and graphic symbol of his rebirth.

In *Landmarks of Healing: A Study of House Made of Dawn*, Susan Scarberry-Garcia links Abel's rubbing of ashes on his upper body, before he joins the dawn runners, with Francisco's bear-hunting story. The act, she notes, is part of a healing ritual and gives Abel the strength and courage of the bear. While earlier in the novel he was unable to sing a creation song of his people, now the words come to him as he runs toward the rising sun, and he sings them loudly. Abel is whole and complete at last.

The Names: A Memoir

Summary and Analysis

Momaday calls *The Names* "an autobiographical account," adding that it is also "an act of the imagination." The book covers the lives of the author's immediate ancestors and his own life from birth to his leaving the Jemez Pueblo in New Mexico for a military academy in Virginia. Just as *House Made of Dawn* is not a conventional novel, so *The Names* is no ordinary memoir: It moves back and forth in time, blending Momaday's personal life story with Kiowa lore and legend and actual historical events. According to Lee Schubnell in his book-length study of Momaday, the memoir's three-part structure is similar to that of the book that preceded it, the multigenre *The Way to Rainy Mountain*.

A brief prologue retells the legend of how the Kiowa, Momaday's people, came to be. Part 1 of the book sets the scene of the author's childhood on the Great Plains near Rainy Mountain Creek and the Washita River in Oklahoma. Momaday focuses on one dramatic memory of childhood, hiding in the storm cellar with his mother during one of the many violent storms that pass through the region.

The narrative then moves back in time to 1850 and the birth of his great-grandmother Nancy Elizabeth in Kentucky. The author quickly moves on to the birth of his maternal grandfather, Theodore, her third child with George Scott, in 1875. Theodore marries Anne Elizabeth Ellis, a woman of European ancestry and four years his senior. Their third child was Momaday's mother, Mayme Natachee, born in 1913.

The focus then shifts to his father's family and his grandfather Mammedaty, a full-blooded Kiowa who Momaday never met. His people subjugated by the U.S. Army, Mammedaty leaves a life of hunting and fighting to become a farmer and has great success. He marries Aho, and they have six children. One son, Huan-toa, is Momaday's father. At his christening, he is given the Christian name Alfred Morris, after a white man who was Mammedaty's good friend. Unlike his father, Alfred decides to leave the land and become an artist and teacher, both ambitions he will eventually achieve. He later takes the name "Momaday" and meets Natachee through the cousin of a friend. They marry in 1933 and live for a time with Alfred's family at Mount View, Oklahoma. The Mammedatys treat Natachee coldly, seeing her as an outsider. Momaday describes his own birth and then imagines a chronicling of the Kiowa people as his great-grandfather Pohd-lohk might have recorded it.

In part 2, the small family (Scott is an only child) leaves Oklahoma and moves to Gallup, New Mexico, in 1936, which Momaday calls "the last frontier town in America." They live at the Navajo reservation at Shiprock where his father gets a job as a truck dispatcher with the roads department of the Indian Service. His mother works as a switchboard operator at the Shiprock Agency and instills a love of literature in Momaday. At one point in the narrative, Momaday writes of himself in the third person, then switches to a first-person narrative before shifting then to the voice of his Uncle James, an alcoholic and a colorful and beloved figure from Momaday's childhood.

In part 3, the family moves again to Hobbs, New Mexico, near an army base. His father finds work as a draftsman for an oil company. Momaday recalls childhood friends, his early school days, and World War II, which had little impact on his young life. "[N]othing of my innocence was lost in it," he writes. Momaday then switches to a long stream-of-consciousness section describing his life in Hobbs. He warns the reader that "One does not pass through time, but time enters upon him, in his place."

In the book's final section, the author flashes forward to when he returns as an adult to Jemez Pueblo outside Albuquerque and the Jemez Day School where his parents taught for more than a quarter century. The school has just burned down, and the event brings back a flood of memories to Momaday, such as when he wrote his first published poem at the desk of a second grader while home from college for a weekend. As a child, Momaday found Jemez, despite the simplicity of life there, a magical place, full of wonder. "It was not our native world," he writes of the Navajos he lived among, "but we appropriated it, as it were, to ourselves; we invested much of our lives in it, and in it was the remembered place of our hopes, our dreams, and our deep love."

Among the vivid recollections Momaday has is of the Feast of San Diego in November when Navajos from all over came to the pueblo to celebrate and be with their people. They came, dressed in colorful clothes, in a seemingly endless caravan of covered wagons. There are other feast days and ceremonies that Momaday recalls, including the bloody chicken pull game that plays a significant role in *House Made of Dawn*.

At age 13, Momaday's parents give him a horse he names Pecos. The long ride he takes on Pecos is symbolic of his entrance into adulthood. "On the back of my horse," he writes, "I had a different view of the world. . . . My mind loomed upon the farthest edges of the earth, where I could feel the full force of the planet whirl-ing through space."

In a brief epilogue, Momaday rides on horseback into a canyon to visit with his elders and then travels to Devils Tower in Wyoming, a sacred place to Indians. He ends his journey near the headwaters of the Yellowstone River where he finds the hollow log from which the Kiowa first emerged at the time of creation. So the story of both Momaday and his people comes, at its end, full circle.

Major Themes

The themes that infuse *The Names* are similar to those the author explores in his other books—both fiction and nonfiction. They include creation and myth, the bicultural world of the Native American today, the power of names, the vital need to re-create the self, and the importance of place in life and the imagination.

The Power of Names

Momaday dedicated his memoir "to those whose names I bear and to those who bear my names." Names are of extreme importance to the Kiowa culture. "[A] man's life proceeds from his name, in the way that a river proceeds from its source," writes the author, quoting Pohd-lohk, his great-grandfather who gave him his Kiowa name, Tsoai-talee, meaning "rock-tree boy." The naming of things is part of the world that children mature into. "Children trust in language," he writes, "creation says to the child: Believe in this tree, for it has a name."

While born with a Christian name, many modern Native Americans fol-low the tradition of their people and undergo a naming ceremony when they are given, as Momaday was, an Indian name. The two names help modern Indians to deal with the two cultures they straddle—modern white-dominated society and the traditional society of their ancestors. "I am," writes Momaday, recalling his naming ceremony. "It is when I am most conscious of being that wonder comes upon my blood, and I want to live forever, and it is no matter that I must die." In the passing down of names from one generation to another, Momaday seems to be saying, there is a suggestion of immortality.

Self-Creation and the Power of the Imagination

Momaday describes his life at times as a journey, a search for his place in the world. While his identification with his people is an important part of his life, he also believes in a re-creation of the self through the individual's creativity and imagination. He points out that about 1929 his mother, who was of mixed heri-tage, began to see herself as an Indian. "This act of the imagination was, I believe, among the most important events of my mother's early life, as later the same es-sential act was to be among the most important of my own," he writes.

What Momaday does not remember or was not exposed to from his past he freely creates out of his imagination, like the life of his grandfather Mammedaty, who he never knew. "He enters into my dreams; he persists in his name," he writes. The mythical creation of the Kiowa that opens and closes the book finds its parallel for Momaday in his own personal myth, drawn from the memories of his childhood. As critic Matthias Schubnell notes, in *The Names*, Momaday "records the process of his symbolic and imaginative identification with his racial heritage."

GERALD VIZENOR

Biography

GERALD VIZENOR is one of the most prolific of contemporary Native American writers. His more than 25 books span a wide range of genres and subjects. He was born on October 22, 1934, in Minneapolis, Minnesota, to a father who was Chippewa and a mother who was Swedish American. His father was murdered when Vizenor was still young, and the crime was never solved. He spent his childhood between foster homes and the White Earth Reservation in northern Minnesota, where he was cared for largely by his father's family. When he was fifteen, Vizenor's stepfather died in a work accident; soon after, the young Gerald lied about his age to enter the Minnesota National Guard. He was honorably discharged before his unit left to serve in the Korean War.

Vizenor joined the army two years later and served in postwar Japan. His exposure to Japanese culture and literature deeply influenced him, and later in his career he would write in the Japanese verse form haiku. Discharged in 1953, Vizenor studied at New York University under the GI Bill and later attended the University of Minnesota, from which he received a bachelor of arts (B.A.) degree in 1960. He continued to attend the university, through 1970, doing graduate work. During this time, he served as a director of the American Indian Employment and Guidance Center in Minneapolis. His experiences with dislocated Native Americans informed his short stories in the collection *Wordarrows: Whites and Indians in the New Fur Trade* (1978). He later became a staff reporter for the *Minneapolis Tribune* and eventually became an editorial contributor. While critical of racist attitudes toward Native Americans, he was also skeptical about many Native American activists who he felt were out to promote themselves and not the interests of their people.

His distinguished career in academia began at Lake Forest College in 1970. He taught at the University of Minnesota (1977–85) and the University of California,

Santa Cruz (1987–90). Vizenor was on the faculty of the University of Oklahoma for one year before moving on to the University of California, Berkeley, in 1991. He currently is professor of American studies at the University of New Mexico.

Vizenor's first novel, *Darkness in Saint Louis Bearheart*, published in 1978, is one of the first science-fiction novels written by a Native American. He revised the work in 1990 under the title *Bearheart: The Heirship Chronicles*. His many other books include works of poetry (*Almost Ashore*, 2006), short stories (*Landfill Meditation: Crossblood Stories,* 1991), nonfiction (*Manifest Manners: Postindian Warriors of Survivance,* 1993) and autobiography (*Interior Landscapes: Autobiographical Myths and Metaphors,* 1990). His novel *Griever: An American Monkey in China* won an American Book Award in 1988. He is also the recipient of the Native Writers' Circle of the Americas 2001 lifetime achievement award.

Vizenor's fiction is filled with outrageous humor, bold imagination, and frequent references to pop culture. Whether writing satirically or realistically, however, he is always serious and earnest when it comes to his thoughts and feelings about the state of Native Americans today.

The Heirs of Columbus
Summary and Analysis

Vizenor's response to the quincentennial of Christopher Columbus's discovery of the Americas in 1992 is an entertaining, if outrageous, mix of historical fiction, fantasy, science fiction, and mystery.

Columbus, in Vizenor's humorous revisionist view, was part Mayan, a man of mixed heritage who was the result of early Mayan exploration of Europe. Columbus goes to North America not to "discover" it but to reclaim his Mayan heritage and revisit his true homeland. He is accompanied by his Mayan lover, Samana.

The novel actually begins in the present, 1992. The central character is Stone Columbus, just one of Columbus's many heirs, who with other descendants has decided to commemorate the quincentennial by establishing a sovereign Native American nation called Point Assinka on Point Roberts in Washington State's Puget Sound. The founders declare Point Assinka a free state with "no prisons, no passports, no public schools, no missionaries, no televisions, and no public taxation." It is an Indian version of utopia with its own symbolic statue in its harbor, not Lady Liberty but "The Trickster of Liberty," a familiar figure in Native American folklore who conquers evil with wit and intelligence.

Stone, in his way, is as prodigious as his famous ancestor. He oversees the Santa Maria Casino, an Indian bingo palace, and is a popular radio talk-show host. The money generated by the casino is used to fund scientific research in genetic surgery, which Vizenor, a lover of invented words, calls "electrophoresis." The heirs see the "leading gene" of the Mayan blood as the world's salvation. Once all people have these genes surgically implanted in their bodies the "genetic code of tribal survivance and radiance" will make the world a better place.

The forces of evil, however, want to stop this program and destroy Point Assinka. Among the novel's chief villains is Doric Miched, who attempts to threaten the heirs by procuring the caskets that hold the remains of Christopher Columbus and Pocahontas, the Indian princess who helped the early Virginia colonists. Doric's plot is thwarted by Felipe Flowers, a self-styled poacher whose mission in life is to recover Indian artifacts from unscrupulous whites. After successfully retrieving Columbus's remains, Flowers is contacted by Pelligrine Treves, an antiquarian book dealer in London, who claims to have the remains of Pocahontas and wants to see them buried in the tribal Home of Life. Flowers goes to Gravesend, England, where the book dealer says the remains are stored in a closet at St. George's Parish Church. When the quest turns out to be a trap, Flowers is abducted, and the anonymous kidnapper calls Stone to make an exchange—Flowers for the remains of Columbus. Before Stone can pay the ransom, however, Flowers's body is discovered at the foot of a statue of Pocahontas at St. George's, the work of the diabolical Miched.

A more supernatural evil is represented by the so-called Evil Gambler, an Indian evil spirit called a *wiindigoo,* who is used by the federal government to disrupt Point Assinka. Federal agents thaw out the water demon who then challenges tribal members to a game of chance in which their lives are at stake. In the final showdown, the future of the world itself hangs in the balance. In the end, however, the Evil Gambler loses his nerve, Miched is arrested and put in prison, and good triumphs over evil. Columbus, Pocahontas, and the courageous Felipe Flowers are all buried on Point Assinka, a reminder of the rich heritage on which this fearless future is built.

Major Themes

Vizenor's wild fantasy touches on many contemporary issues that matter to Native Americans today: Indian gambling, tribal sovereignty, the fight between tribes and white institutions for Native American remains and artifacts, and the conflicting revisions of historical fact. While Vizenor uses humor and parody in his fiction, his attacks on the forces he sees as diminishing Native American life and culture are resolutely serious.

Revising History

At the outset, Vizenor's revisionist view of Columbus and his achievements is absurd. On closer examination, however, there is a point behind the levity. Vizenor shows his readers that making Columbus a Mayan is no less absurd than some of the other revisionist takes on exploration and colonization. Every historian is a product of his or her time and place and is influenced by bias and personal ideology. There is, Vizenor seems to be saying, no "objective" version of the past. The writer's political agenda will determine how he views history, whether it is the story of Columbus or any of the other explorers and colonizers who came after him to the Americas.

History, in the end, is just another story told to people. The stories that Stone and his heirs tell their native people are meant to give them pride and an identity that cannot be taken from them. The authorities see their sovereign state as a threat and try to steal the story from them, whether it be literally, by stealing the actual remains of their heroes, or metaphorically stealing their souls through gambling and the rampant greed and materialism that it represents in the world today.

The Figure of the Trickster

The trickster, usually represented by a rabbit or other animal in Indian folklore, is a potent figure in the fiction of Gerald Vizenor and crops up in many of his novels and stories. As one character states in Vizenor's first novel, *Darkness in Saint Louis Bearheart*, "The tricksters and warriorclowns have stopped more evil violence with their wit than have lovers with their lust and fools with their power and rage . . ." Unlike other heroes in myth and legend, the trickster relies on wit and cunning to defeat evil forces, not brute strength or invincible weapons. Evil is rarely vanquished in the world of Native American literature, only defeated temporarily. The trickster must be ever vigilant for its return.

The trickster, like Stone Columbus in the novel, is also a storyteller. The stories do not merely amuse and entertain but bring people together, heal wounds, and bind communities.

Chancers
Summary and Analysis

This novel, published in 2000, takes place on the campus of the University of California at Berkeley where two groups are vying for power in the native studies program. The Solar Dancers are a band of outlaw students, who under the power of the cannibalistic *wiindigoo*, a supernatural monster, are systematically and sacrificially killing college administrators and exchanging their skulls for native bones in order to release spirit "chancers," resurrected deceased native peoples, and return them to life. They are led by students with such names as Token White, Fast Food, Injun Time, Cloud Burst, and Bad Mouth. The Solar Dancers are opposed by the Round Dancers, led by Peter Roses (also referred to as Round Dance), the dean of native studies, who argues against the Solar Dancers' "ideologies of victimry." His message centers on the liberating power of erotic love.

The novel, as with most of Vizenor's fiction, is filled with outrageous characters. There is Pardone de Cozner (also known as Cozzie White Mouth) who lectures on casino and tribal law at the university, while running a successful chicken-plucking factory on the side with his partner, Mannie Medicine, a transvestite who operates a rental service for inflatable blondes. Then there is Ruby Blue Welcome, a woman of Creek and Seminole heritage, who is dean of native admissions and gives lectures on native religions with the help of her hand puppet, Four Skins. Ruby Blue is carrying on a tempestuous affair with Dr. Paul Snow (also called Snow Boy), senior osteologist at the university's Phoebe Hearst Museum of Anthropology, who can only be sexually aroused by the native skeletons that are his stock and trade. Sex and violence dominate the action of this savagely satirical novel, as one by one, provosts and college officials mysteriously disappear.

The narrator is a native lecturer and novelist who looks to Roses as his mentor. The pivotal character, though, is Token White, the only non-native Solar Dancer, who is a talented archer and enamored of the music of Johnny Cash. To prove her devotion to the native cause, Token White participates in a Ghost Dance in which the flesh is torn from her chest. After seeing Snow and Ruby Blue making love, Token White, a kind of angel of death, kills them with two well-placed arrows from her bow. Four Skins is "kidnapped" by the Solar Dancers and dismembered.

Characters from other Vizenor novels also appear, including Conk Browne, a visiting lecturer on native transmotion and visionary sovereignty and an expert on elevators, and her aunt Tulip Browne, a private investigator who is hired to look into the murders. Conk possesses the bones of Pocahontas, the legendary native woman who traveled to England in the early seventeenth century; she calls her "sister."

When Pardone conspires to overthrow the Round Dancers and take control of native studies by using the Solar Dancers, he is put on trial by his allies, who insist he is not a real Indian. He is ardently defended by his enemy, Roses, who declares, "Cloud Burst and the solar dancers are the victims, the round dancers are the erotic visionaries, and our own stinky chicken plucker is the perfect clown and scapegoat. Now that, my friends, creates the sacred in native studies." The reckless liberties undertaken by the Solar Dancers prompts Provost Greene (one of the few left alive on campus) to declare the termination of native studies at the end of the academic year.

Commencement for the program is held in the Mather Redwood Grove and promises a showdown between the two feuding groups. The Solar Dancers set the redwoods on fire with their cigars and are taken to the hospital after suffering from smoke inhalation. Token White is the only Solar Dancer remaining and the only one who will graduate. When the Solar Dancers return, several chancers appear on the podium including the resurrected Pocahontas and Four Skins, who is manipulated by Mannie Medicine until he is shot with arrows and set on fire. Token White, feeling betrayed by her comrades, shoots the remaining Solar Dancers with arrows. "What a time this has been," says one of the surviving characters. "Everybody hoppy?" asks another.

Major Themes

The freewheeling comedy of this and other Vizenor novels does not endear him to all readers. There are no real, three- (or often even two-) dimensional characters to identify or sympathize with. The frantic pace and cartoonish sexual and violent behavior of the outlandish characters is highly satirical and intentionally so. Nonetheless, Vizenor's perverse perspectives and black humor are not without their purpose, as they are the author's means of eliciting insights about the modern world, intellectual pursuits, and Native American attitudes.

The satire is directed at such characters as Pardone and Ruby Blue, who use Native American heritage to their own ends, and at the dedicated natives (represented by the Solar Dancers) who see themselves as romantic rebels, modeling themselves after their mystical ancestors. Vizenor has little patience for either camp. Where his allegiance lies is at times unclear. The Round Dancers are manipulators in their own way, but at least they do not see themselves as victims or activists. The best revenge on life, Vizenor seems to suggest, may lie not in seeing oneself as a victim or a master but in engaging life freely and to the fullest.

Satire of Native American Activists

Vizenor has been the adversary of political activists since his days as a journalist when he questioned the motives of members of the American Indian Movement (AIM). What Vizenor perceived to be the activists' egotism and opportunism are embodied in the outrageous behavior of the Solar Dancers. In his summary of the complaints against the native students, Provost Greene condemns the number of long-distance calls charged to the department by students. "Dependence on the oral tradition is no longer an acceptable explanation for so many expensive long-distance calls," he says.

The mystique and sexual prowess of the "warrior" is caricatured in the hand puppet Four Skins. Vizenor makes the point that the image fashioned of the Native American by the Solar Dancers is no more valid or reflective of reality than those created by a racist white society. "Tell me, how is your invention any different from the *Indians* we invented all over the world and right out back on mother earth," says one white character to the Solar Dancers, "the same mother you polluted with everyone else?"

Truth in Storytelling

For all his dark humor, Vizenor is not without a positive or serious point to make. The stories that Round Dance uses to enthrall his "blondes" are important and necessary. The narrator has encrypted electronic narratives that ethnic emissaries use to create more extended narratives for thousands of subscribers around the world. These stories from the past are essential in giving people a sense of identity and purpose. This is the purpose of the chancers as well.

"The emissaries are dead voices on the monitor, and my stories go on," says the nameless narrator, "they must go on, in the silence and shadow of words, or so it seems in the world of native chancers. How much do we simulate at the crossover of sound and scripture the words to name our presence?" In Vizenor's madcap fictive world, words and the stories they tell form a living, fluid tradition and a source of stability and meaning.

JAMES WELCH

Biography

ONE OF THE FOUNDING FATHERS of the Native American renaissance, James Welch never achieved the exposure or widespread popularity enjoyed by some of his contemporaries. Yet he wrote movingly and memorably about Native American life and experience, both past and present. He was born in Browning, Montana, on November 18, 1940. His father was Blackfeet, and his mother belonged to the Gros Ventre tribe. For much of his early life, he lived with his family on the Fort Belknap Reservation in Montana.

Welch's desire to write led him to attend the University of Montana, where he studied creative writing with poet Richard Hugo, who became his mentor. At Hugo's urging, Welch began to write about the things he knew—reservation life and Native American culture. His first novel, *Winter in the Blood* (1974), was critically acclaimed, as was his second, *The Death of Jim Loney* (1979). His epic historical novel *Fools Crow* (1986) earned him an American Book Award. Welch also wrote poetry (*Riding the Earthboy 40,* 1976) and nonfiction (*Killing Custer: The Battle of Little Bighorn and the Fate of the Plains Indians* with Paul Stekler, 1995).

Although underappreciated in the United States, Welch was a popular literary figure in Europe through translations of his novels. In 2000, he was knighted in France for his service to French culture. His last published work, *The Heartsong of Charging Elk*, another historical novel about an Ogallala Sioux who worked in Buffalo Bill's Wild West Show, appeared in 2000. Welch, who contracted lung cancer, died of a heart attack at age 62 at his home in Missoula, Montana, on August 4, 2003.

A prose writer of great style and precision, Welch wrote in a more traditional, straightforward narrative style than N. Scott Momaday and other Native American writers. The darkness of his vision of contemporary Indian life was often softened by his keen sense of humor and optimistic outlook on human nature.

Winter in the Blood
Summary and Analysis

The protagonist and narrator of James Welch's first novel is a nameless 32-year-old Blackfeet Indian who lives with Teresa, his mother, on a ranch at the Fort Belknap Reservation in Montana. His life is as desolate as the winter of the title. He feels alienated from his self-centered mother, his grandmother who seldom speaks, and his new stepfather, Lame Bull, who marries Teresa during a three-day spree. The narrator's father, John First Raise, died ten years earlier, freezing to death while walking home drunk from a bar. The narrator's girlfriend, Agnes, a Cree Indian, has left him at the novel's start, taking his gun and electric razor with her.

The plot, slim as it is, centers on the narrator's search for Agnes. In the first of the novel's four parts, he takes the bus to the nearby town of Malta and meets up with Agnes's untrustworthy brother Dougie. Dougie convinces the narrator to help him rob a drunken white man. The narrator agrees and then hides out in a hotel, fearing the white man will remember him and come looking for him.

In part 2, the narrator is back on the ranch. He rides his horse, Bird, which he has owned since childhood, to the home of Yellow Calf, an old blind Indian who was a friend of his father's. The anonymous protagonist then goes to a bar with Lame Bull, who is enjoying his role as master of the ranch. He meets an older woman name Malvina who offers him a ride to Havre, another nearby town, where he hopes to find Agnes. He spends the night on Malvina's couch; in the morning, when she rejects his sexual advances, he leaves. In downtown Havre, he meets up again with a man known only as the "airplane man." The most mysterious character in the novel, the airplane man is more confused and alienated than even the narrator is. The man is a fugitive from his former life, which he sparingly discusses in an ever-changing story. He tells the narrator that he has absconded with money that is not his and is running away from the Federal Bureau of Investigation (FBI). He asks the narrator to drive him across the border into Canada, enticing him by saying the narrator can keep the car that the airplane man will buy after he returns to Montana. The narrator agrees to the plan and then goes to find Agnes who he sighted in front of a saloon. He tries to make amends with Agnes, but she is noncommittal and warns him that her brother Dougie is looking for him with the intention of beating him up. There seems to be little motive for Dougie's actions, other than to get the narrator before he gets him. Their conversation is interrupted when someone, presumably Dougie, arrives and delivers a crushing punch to the narrator, leaving him in the street with a bloody nose.

Out in the street, the narrator sees the police arrest the airplane man, possibly for embezzlement. A woman named Marlene empathizes with the narrator and his bloodied nose, and he gives her money to buy him some wine. His ego and his body bruised, he meets up with Marlene and spends the night with her in a hotel room. The narrator is unsatisfied with their sexual encounter, striking her in the face when she seeks intimacy from him, and leaves.

"I had had enough of Havre," he says as part 2 draws to a close, "enough of town, of walking home, hung over, beaten up, or both. I had had enough of the people, the bartenders, the bars, the cars, the hotels, but mostly I had had enough of myself. I wanted to lose myself . . ."

In part 3, he hitches a ride home to the reservation. The ranch is empty, not even his grandmother is there to greet him. He presumes, correctly, that she has died. He has little reaction to her death, helping Lame Bull to dig her grave on their property, a common Indian custom.

His grandmother's death conjures memories of Mose, his older brother who died several years earlier. He finally recalls the events leading up to Mose's death in vivid detail, which Welch describes in a rich style, in sharp contrast to the terse, simple prose that dominates the rest of the narrative. At age twelve, the narrator was rounding up stray cows with Mose, two years his senior, when his horse, Bird, ran across the highway to catch a stray. Mose followed and was struck by a car and killed. The narrator has felt at least partly responsible for his brother's death. By revisiting the painful event, he is unburdened of the guilt and feels he can move on with his life.

In part 4, the protagonist visits old Yellow Calf again to tell him about the grandmother's death. The old man relates her story, which the narrator heard only part of from the old woman herself. At age twenty, she married an older chief. During an especially trying winter, the Chief died. The rest of the tribe felt the grandmother was responsible for his death and subsequently shunned her. Only one warrior came to her assistance and became her hunter and protector. That man, the narrator now realizes, was Yellow Calf. The old man is Teresa's father and the narrator's grandfather. The narrator now knows something of his personal story and is grateful for it. Knowing at last where he came from gives him the courage to face the future.

This renewed spirit is dramatically displayed when the narrator finds a cow trapped in mud. He ties a rope to the helpless animal and struggles to pull it out astride Bird. The strain kills the old horse, but the cow is freed and reunited with its calf. The narrator has gone from being a passive drifter, wandering aimlessly through his existence, to a person who takes an active role in the struggle of life.

In the novel's brief epilogue, the narrator joins his mother and Lame Bull at his grandmother's burial service. As Lame Bull delivers a simple eulogy beside her grave, the narrator resolves to forge ahead on his life's path. His winter has given way to the expectation and hope of spring.

Major Themes

Winter in the Blood is a deceptively simple story. Welch has skillfully used a sparse, episodic style to describe the narrator's wintry world of desolation and despair. Only when he describes the stories of his grandmother and Yellow Calf and the death of Mose does the author's style become rich and textured, exposing the depth of feeling the young man is experiencing at these moments.

The novel, albeit brief in length, is rich in thematic resonance. Central themes include the dislocation and alienation of contemporary Native Americans, redemption from guilt, disintegration of the family unit, and the difficulty of sustaining relationships.

Breakdown of the Family

The disintegration of the narrator's life is closely tied to the lack of connection he feels with his family. His father and brother, both long dead, are shadowy figures in his recollections. His mother is cold and unresponsive, and his new stepfather is wrapped up in his own self-importance. Agnes, who has spent three weeks living in their house, is mistaken for the narrator's wife by his mother and grandmother, a misidentification that he does not bother to correct. Welch equates the narrator's lack of family unity with all that is wrong in his life. In a larger sense, the breakdown of the family is the breakdown of the generations, of the traditional lifeways of the Blackfeet nation that produced him. "He [the narrator] is ineffective in relationships with people and at odds with his environment," observes Kathleen M. Sands in an essay on the novel, "not because he is deliberately rebellious, or even immaturely selfish, but because he has lost the story of who he is, where he has come from."

The airplane man is a symbol of the limits of modern man's alienation. He is a solitary figure, fleeing his family, without friends and without direction. The outrageous stories he tells the narrator may be true or false, but either way his life is a dead end, one that the narrator will hopefully learn from and avoid.

The Redemptive Power of Stories

While the airplane man's stories are chaotic and incomplete, other narrative voices lead the protagonist back to discovering and embracing his identity. Yellow Calf's tale of tribal life in an earlier age and the role his grandmother played in it gives the young man the solidity of a definable background and thus adds reason and purpose to his life. Together the old man and his grandson laugh as they recognize the significance of the moment: "And so we shared this secret in the presence of ghosts, in wind that called for the muttering tepees, the blowing snow, the white air of the horses' nostrils. The cottonwood behind us, their dead white branches angling to the threatening clouds, sheltered these ghosts as they had sheltered the camp that winter."

Later, when the narrator meets neighbors who offer their sympathies at his grandmother's death, he creates his own story. He tells them his "wife" has returned and even invites them to see her at the ranch. His lie has purpose and shows that he desires marriage, the stability of family, and the responsibilities that go with it. "Next time I'd do it right," he thinks in the closing lines of the novel. "Buy her a couple of crèmes de menthe, maybe offer to marry her on the spot." It is a tentative stab at responsibility, but one that may lead to something more solid and permanent. To bind his past to his present, the narrator throws his traditional pouch into the open grave of his grandmother.

The Death of Jim Loney
Summary and Analysis

Welch's second novel is the grim story of Jim Loney, a young man who, as his name suggests, is a loner. Half white and half Indian, he feels part of neither group. As Welch writes: "He had no family and he wasn't Indian or white. He remembered the day he and Rhea [his girlfriend] had driven out to the Little Rockies. She had said he was lucky to have two sets of ancestors. In truth he had none."

As part 1 of the novel opens, Loney is seen attending a local football game in the small Montana town he calls home. After, he goes to a bar where an Indian friend Russell is the bartender. It is quickly made clear that Russell is bothered by Loney's lack of interest in anything. While others enter into and embrace life, Loney merely sits on the sidelines, watching with disinterest the same way he passively observed the football game. Russell boasts of marrying a woman named Estelle Pipe and is surprised when Loney tells him he has a girlfriend now too. She is 29-year-old Rhea, a well-educated white woman from a wealthy Dallas family who works as a local schoolteacher. Disillusioned by life in Montana where she hoped to find herself, Rhea has come to love Loney, although his lack of any initiative frustrates her as well. He works for a local farmer but spends much of his time lazing and drinking alcohol. He has recurrent dreams of a dark bird hovering over and calling to him. In his other repeating dream, he meets a strange woman who is looking for her lost son in a graveyard.

Loney is truly alone in the world. His Indian mother, Electra Calf-Looking, abandoned him and his sister, Kate, early in life and their white father, Ike, an alcoholic and a derelict, eventually walked out on his children as well. Loney was raised for a few years by a woman named Sandra, who he believes was an aunt. She was the only person who seemed to care about him. He later learns from his sister that Sandra was the woman his father lived with after their mother left and that she took in Jim after his father left her as well. Unlike Jim, Kate has made something of her life and has an important job in Washington, D.C. She is coming to visit him at the conclusion of part 1.

In part 2, Kate has arrived after a long delay in her flight, and Loney introduces her to Rhea. The two women immediately like each other, although Kate cannot fathom what a woman of Rhea's background can see in her brother, who she refers to as "a man almost devoid of tangible qualities." She feels that Rhea will soon tire of Jim and go back to Dallas and the world she left behind. When they are alone, Kate invites Jim to come back with her to Washington, D.C., to start a new life, but it is clear that he has no intentions of leaving Montana.

Meanwhile, their absent father, Ike, has returned to town and is hanging out with his old friend Kenny Hart, who runs another local bar. Painter Barthelme, a former high school classmate of Loney who played basketball with him on a winning team, is also introduced. Barthelme took a different path than Jim and is now a tribal police officer. He met Rhea during a classroom police visit and has fallen for her. Another of Jim's classmates, the threatening Myron Pretty Weasel, also returns to town. He and Jim go drinking in Kenny's bar where they meet Rhea and her fellow teacher Colleen. Loney and Rhea talk outside in her car about the future. Rhea is planning to move to Seattle and wants Jim to go with her, but again any plan of change or relocation is met with Jim's resistance. Although he loves Rhea in his own way, he feels he can offer her nothing.

The next morning, Pretty Weasel shows up at Loney's ramshackle home and tells him they are going hunting. Loney resists at first but finally agrees to join him. Pretty Weasel is the aggressive Indian, slightly dangerous and violence prone, that Loney refuses to become. On the hunt, they spy a bear, a rare animal to see in the area. They split up as they stalk the animal and, blinded by sunlight, Loney accidentally shoots his friend, killing him.

In part 3, Loney has returned to town and is trying to reach Kate, who is back in Washington, D.C., but he is unable to contact her. Rhea has packed and, despite the pleas of her friend Colleen to stay, plans to leave town the next day, still hoping that Loney might join her.

Loney goes to the trailer where his father is living, and the two finally meet. Loney has come to learn the truth about his mother and his past. After initially calling her a whore, Ike admits that Electra was a good woman, but that they were not happy with each other. Loney confesses to his father that he has shot Pretty Weasel and is not sure if it was an accident or that he killed his friend intentionally. Ironically, for the first time Ike becomes animated and fatherly, thrusting $60 in cash and a rifle on Loney to help him get away before he is caught by the police. Loney refuses the money but takes the gun. Before he leaves, he asks his father if they each "could have done something," realized more successful lives, if Ike had not abandoned the family when he did. Ike's callous but honest reply is, " . . . what would we have done but drink ourselves to death?"

Loney's frustration at the world and his father is exhibited when he leaves the trailer and uses the rifle to shoot out a window, perhaps meaning to hit Ike. Loney then goes to see Rhea one last time. "'I do love you,' she said, her voice drifting.

And he almost said it too, but there was no place to take it." The next morning, as he prepares to leave, Loney reviews his life and searches for a reason why he has become the numb, detached individual he now is. "Somewhere along the line he had started questioning his life and he had lost forever the secret of survival," Welch writes.

Ike, who was cut by the shattered glass from the rifle shot the night before, has called the police and, happy to be the center of attention for once in his life, betrays his son. He tells them Loney has killed Pretty Weasel whose body has not yet been discovered and tells them they can find his son in nearby Mission Canyon. Painter Barthelme is one of the officers. Quinton Doore, who was also a member of their high school basketball team, is the other policeman on the scene. Unlike Painter, Doore seems to have forsaken his empathy for his fellow Indians, growing hardened in his authoritative role among his people.

Loney goes to Mission Canyon, waiting for the police to arrive. When they do, Painter realizes that everything Loney has done is meant to lead to his capture or death. Doore takes aim and fires at Loney who is fully exposed to them. The novel ends with this sentence: "And he fell, and as he was falling he felt a harsh wind where there was none and the last thing he saw were the beating wings of a dark bird as it climbed to a distant place."

Major Themes

Rhea describes Jim Loney at one point in the novel as suffering "a crisis of spirit." A sense of hopelessness and meaninglessness permeates the novel. The themes of alienation and death, both physical and spiritual, are the most prominent. Love and its limitations, a sense of place, and the breakdown of family life emerge as central thematic concerns as well.

Spiritual and Physical Death

The title of the novel seems to doom the protagonist from the start. Although he is shot and killed at the end of the book, Jim Loney is spiritually dead and numb to the world from the moment he is introduced. The only people he relates to—his lover, Rhea, and his sister, Kate—try to pull him back into a meaningful life, but they both fail, despite the love they have for him.

Death haunts the novel and the central character. Other deaths mirror his own. Loney's dog Swipsey dies, frozen in ice. He learns of the death of Sandra, Ike's former lover, from his sister. He tells Pretty Weasel about the death of George Yellow Eyes, the star of their high school basketball team, who died in an accident in another town. To everyone else, George Yellow Eyes simply disappeared. Only Loney knew what really happened to him. Like Yellow Eyes, Loney longs to simply disappear from life.

His climactic meeting with his father is initially prompted by a desperate need to learn about his past and forge a meaningful identity, but it ends with the fulfillment of his death wish. He tells his father about his crime and then tells him exactly where he is going to go, Mission Canyon, knowing that the old man will betray him to the police.

Loney waits for them to arrive in the canyon and when they do, Painter, who is the protagonist's foil, comes to the realization that he has no intention of escaping from them. "Painter read the signs," Welch writes, "but he didn't know why Loney would do this. There are odd things that people do, he thought, things done out of a need that defies an ordinary man's reasoning." Doore, on the other hand, understands Loney's motivations and reasoning and is ready to serve as his angel of death, shooting him twice.

In death, Loney finally finds the peace that had eluded him. Death is a welcome release from a life that is meaningless and painful. The dark bird that he watches as it "climbed to a distant place" may signal a better afterlife for Jim Loney, but it offers slim hope in a novel of persistent gloom and unrelieved pessimism.

The Search for Self-Identity

As numbed to life as he is, Loney still has a desire to know himself and, for him, this quest for identity means knowing where he came from. He is obsessed with Sandra, the woman who raised him as a child, and plies Kate with questions about her. Kate has managed to create a new identity for herself by leaving the family and community behind. She did not want to live with Sandra as a child and shows little interest in their father who has returned to town after a long absence. Loney, in contrast, actively seeks out his father, meeting up with him at the trailer he calls home. It is the stories of the past, especially the life and fate of his mother that Loney has come to hear. However, unlike Yellow Calf, the grandfather in *Winter in the Blood*, Ike is an unreliable keeper of stories, and his narrative about Loney's mother is broken, fragmented, and unsatisfying. Loney's desire to hear the story that could make him whole goes unfulfilled, and he leaves the trailer ready to face his own death.

Fools Crow
Summary and Analysis

After two short contemporary novels, James Welch produced this epic, historical novel about his ancestors living in the 1870s as their way of life was about to change forever. The central character is Fools Crow, a young Blackfoot man, who belongs to a tribe called the Lone Eaters.

At the novel's start, Fools Crow is called White Man's Dog and is looked down on by his contemporaries, viewed as a weak individual. His friend Fast Horse invites him to participate in a horse raid against their rivals, the Crows. Yellow Kidney, the leader of the raid, puts White Man's Dog in charge of the group that will actually steal the horses. The raid is successful, until a Crow scout spots the raiding party. White Man's Dog kills the scout, but the other two leaders show poor judgment.

Fast Horse mocks and threatens the Crow in a loud voice, jeopardizing the entire operation. Yellow Kidney is almost captured and hides in a Crow lodge. He lies down next to a Crow woman and has a sexual encounter with her during the night. Only later does he realize his mistake: The woman has smallpox. Yellow Kidney does not contract the disease, but he is captured and tortured by the Crow. They cut off his fingers and then send him into a snowstorm, tied to the back of a horse.

White Man's Dog avoids a similar fate and, after returning to the village, is hailed as a hero. Fast Horse leaves the tribe in disgrace and joins a renegade party led by Owl Child that attacks and kills white settlers, which the Blackfeet call Napikwans.

White Man's Dog earns the name Fools Crow when he scalps the Crow chief Bull Shield. Fools Crow marries Red Paint, the daughter of Yellow Kidney, who has returned to the tribe. He further solidifies his reputation as a great warrior and leader when he kills a Napikwan who is an aggressive hunter of the wild game the Blackfeet depend on for survival. In the mortal struggle, Fools Crow is wounded by a gunshot. The cycle of killing and revenge continues. Yellow Kidney, who has gone off to be on his own, is shot and killed by a Napikwan seeking vengeance on Owl Child's party of marauders. Fools Crow proves his skill as a healer as well as a warrior, when he cures Red Paint's brother of rabies, after the young man is bitten by a wolf.

In the last section of the novel, Fools Crow visits the Feather Woman, a mythical figure and daughter of the Sun and Morning Star. She shows him four visions of the future, all of which spell destruction and death for the Blackfeet's world at the hands of the encroaching whites and the diseases they bring with them. Feather Woman urges Fools Crow to prepare his people for the difficult times to come. He starts passing on the stories of the Blackfeet to the next generation. Near the novel's end, the Marias Massacre of 1870 takes place, when innocent Blackfeet were slaughtered by members of the U.S. Cavalry. Despite the death and graphic violence depicted in this section, the book concludes on a hopeful note. Those Blackfeet who survive adapt their lives and manage to survive in the new society of whites. Their proud descendants live on today.

Major Themes

Although historical fiction, *Fools Crow* does not take the more conventional viewpoint of the war between the Native Americans and the U.S. Army in the nineteenth century. Welch chooses to find a happier ending in his chronicle than many writers and historians have before him. "Although the book skirts tragedy," writes Alan Velie in a perceptive essay, "it ends on a positive, indeed triumphant and defiant note, the hallmark of romance."

Throughout this epic work, the author weaves in such important themes as confrontation versus accommodation, history as divine plan, and the role of the hero and leader in history.

Conflict Versus Accommodation

Some Native American writers have viewed the struggle of their people to retain their land and lives as a noble resistance. Welch takes a somewhat different view. His protagonist, while he fights when necessary, is not a warrior first. Early on, when he kills the Crow scout during the horse raid, Fools Crow comes to regret the death, even though the dead man is a sworn enemy. Violence only begets more violence, as is made clear when the acts of terror carried out by Owl Child's band of renegades reverberates with acts of revenge from the whites.

Fools Crow comes to see the futility of this tactic and becomes a negotiator and accommodator. Welch in no way sees this as a coward's way to avoid a fight. He stresses the important of negotiating with the whites from a position of strength. The critical thing seems to be to know when to stop fighting and start negotiating while the tribe still has power. This approach is shown to be successful by Welch when he recounts the history of the Blackfeet who, like his own ancestors, became successful ranchers and farmers. As one character in the novel says, "the Blackfeet must cut the best bargain they can. They owe it to their children. The tribe must survive."

How high the price of that survival is for contemporary Native Americans is a theme explored in other books and by other authors. In *Fools Crow*, Welch chooses to celebrate the past not as a dead end but as a bridge for his people to the present and the future.

Human History as Divine Plan

In the last part of *Fools Crow*, Welch turns to the mythic figure of the Feather Woman to guide Fools Crow. A transgressor of the laws of the gods, Feather Woman is banished as punishment for breaking a taboo, a fate that extends as well to her people, the Blackfeet. The exile, however, is temporary, and she will return to favor as will the Blackfeet. This vision of a promising future gives Fools Crow and his tribe the courage and confidence to carry on in the face of overwhelming tragedy, such as the bloody massacre that occurs near the novel's end. In Welch's worldview, history is not a series of missteps and accidents but part of a divine plan.

This same theory infuses the work of many nineteenth-century historians who saw history as divinely driven and as a progression from chaos to civilization. It took two world wars in the following century to prompt many thinkers and writers to question this progression. Yet for Welch, this vision of history as being driven by a divine plan is a positive approach that can bind the wounds of the past and engage his people, giving them an identity to carry proudly into a better future.

MICHAEL DORRIS

Biography

A WRITER WHO BURST ONTO the literary scene with two highly praised volumes of fiction and memoir, Michael Dorris was one of the most admired of Native American writers before a family scandal destroyed his career and drove him to a tragic death.

He was born in Louisville, Kentucky, on January 30, 1945, to a Modoc father and a mother of Irish and French ancestry. (His paternal ancestry has never been documented.) While still a child, his father committed suicide, and Michael was raised by his mother and an aunt. A good student, Dorris attended Georgetown University in Washington, D.C., graduating with a B.A. degree in 1967. He went on to earn a master's of philosophy degree from Yale University in 1970. Dorris taught briefly at Franconia College in New Hampshire before being hired by Dartmouth College to run their new Native American studies department in 1972.

The previous year, Dorris, at age 26, became the first unmarried man in the United States to adopt a child, a three-year-old Lakota boy, Reynold Abel, who was later diagnosed with fetal alcohol syndrome (FAS), a chronic condition that severely limited his mental and physical abilities. Dorris movingly wrote about his relationship with Abel in his second book, *The Broken Cord* (1989). He later adopted two more Native American children—Jeffrey Sava in 1974 and Madeline in 1976.

In 1981, Dorris married his former student Louise Erdrich. Together they had three more children, all girls. Dorris and Erdrich inspired each other in their writing, often collaborating and editing each other's work. Dorris's first novel, *A Yellow Raft in Blue Water* (1987), was hailed by many critics as one of the best novels of the decade. *The Broken Cord* was received with similar praise by the critics and earned a National Book Critics Circle Award. Erdrich achieved similar fame with her first novel, *Love Medicine* (1984). Dorris's reputation continued to grow, although none of his succeeding novels were judged to be the equal of his first.

In 1995, Dorris's life began to unravel. His adopted son Sava (Reynold was killed in an automobile accident four years earlier) accused him and Erdrich of child abuse. Soon after, difficulties in what many thought was the perfect marriage of literary idols began to surface, and the couple separated and eventually began divorce proceedings.

Unable to stand the anguish of their separation, Dorris unsuccessfully attempted suicide at the New Hampshire farmhouse where he was living. Soon after, two of his biological daughters accused him of sexual abuse while the family was living in Minnesota. Fearing his reputation would never recover from the charges, which he denied, Dorris told a friend, "My life is over." On the night of April 10, 1997, he committed suicide in a motel room in Concord, New Hampshire, by a combination of drugs, alcohol, and suffocation. At his former wife's request, all records of the investigation against him were permanently sealed.

"I hope his legacy will not be about his suicide and the disturbing allegations, but about how he spent 30 years building Native American literature and studies," said his friend Douglas Foster soon after Dorris's death. "He was a model of the socially engaged writer."

A Yellow Raft in Blue Water
Summary and Analysis

Michael Dorris's first and, by general consensus, his best novel is the story of three generations of Native American women—Ida, matriarch of a troubled family; Christine, her wayward daughter; and Rayona, her granddaughter, struggling to make her way in a cold, alienating world. Each of the novel's three sections is told by one of these protagonists. As the novel progresses, a full picture of who these women are and the courage they possess assembles for the reader.

The first section is narrated by Rayona, who visits her unconventional mother in a hospital in Washington State where she is seriously ill. They are joined briefly by Rayona's father, the irresponsible Elgin, who is black. Elgin has come to return Christine's car but will not stay, despite her illness. As sick as she is, Christine decides to leave the hospital without permission and drive to the Montana reservation where she grew up and where her mother, Ida, still lives. Ray accompanies her, but when they find Ida, who insists on being called "aunt" and not "mother," Christine cannot face her and flees. Rayona stays on and lives with "Aunt Ida," who sends her to the mission school on the reservation.

Rayona does not get along with most of the other young Indians she meets at school, but she is befriended by Father Tom, a local priest. Father Tom's intentions are suspect when he invites Rayona to drive with him to a weekend Christian jamboree. Along the way, they stop to rest at a campground with a lake where Rayona swims out to the raft of the book's title. Father Tom clumsily attempts to seduce her, fails, and in a bout of guilt, gives her money to take the train to visit her father in Seattle. Rayona takes the money but does not take the train. Instead, she stays at the campground and befriends Sky (also known as Norman), an easy-going former 1960s draft dodger who runs the local gas station. Sky introduces Rayona to his wife, Evelyn, a waitress at the local diner, who helps her find a temporary job as a park maintenance worker. The couple invites Rayona to live in their trailer as a tenant, and she becomes a surrogate daughter to them.

Sky and Evelyn soon learn the truth about Rayona and take her to a rodeo where she meets up with her cousin Foxy, a bronco rider. Foxy is too drunk to compete in the rodeo, and Rayona ends up taking his place in the bronco-riding competition. She does surprisingly well and wins a silver belt as a prize. Being awarded the belt is a turning point in Rayona's life: She has proved herself and has earned a distinction to be proud of. After the rodeo, Sky, Evelyn, and Ray meet up with Dayton, another Indian and an old friend of Christine's. Dayton agrees to take Rayona to see her mother, who is living with him. Realizing she is in good hands, Sky and Evelyn depart. Christine and Rayona are reunited but not immediately reconciled. The morning after Ray's arrival at Dayton's, the mother and daughter talk. Christine tells Ray about her childhood and how she lost her faith back in 1960.

In part 2 of the book, the narration shifts to Christine who recalls growing up on the Montana reservation with her mother and younger brother, Lee, whom she idolized. Christine is boy crazy and highly social, but the one boy whose attention she cannot seem to capture is Dayton, Lee's best friend. Both Lee and Dayton refuse to enlist in the military to fight in the Vietnam War. Christine cannot accept this and pressures her brother to join, telling him he will never achieve the leadership role in the tribe he is so richly suited for, if he does not serve. With Dayton's help, Christine finally persuades her brother to enlist.

Soon after, Christine leaves for Seattle to pursue a new job. While there, Dayton informs her that Lee is reported missing in action. Distressed and feeling guilty, Christine goes to a bar to drink away her troubles and is surprised to discover it is a bar with a black clientele. Elgin, a black soldier on leave, picks her up. Christine goes home with him, and they begin a relationship. When Elgin finally completes his hitch in the service, he and Christine move to Tacoma, where Elgin gets a job as a mail carrier. They marry, and Christine becomes pregnant. Elgin quickly loses interest in his wife and starts pursuing other women. When Christine gives birth to Rayona, Elgin makes an attempt to be a better husband and father, but the relationship continues to deteriorate.

Lee's body is soon found, and Christine returns home to the reservation with her baby to attend his funeral and burial. Her relationship with her mother, Ida, is still unresolved, but Ida seems to have no problem accepting her child into the family. Christine moves back to Seattle and continues to have an on-and-off relationship with Elgin. She later becomes ill and ends up in the hospital. There, she is told by her doctors that hard living has taken its toll on her body and that, at age 41, she is dying. In the hospital, Christine relates the events witnessed at the novel's beginning, only told from her perspective. Running away from Ida's was not simply a selfish act on her part, rather she wanted Rayona to stay with her grandmother, because Christine was incapable of caring for her. Christine then moves in with Dayton, who accepts her unconditionally. Dayton has also suffered as an outsider. A teacher, he was wrongfully accused of molesting a male student and was fired from his job. We again see the final reconciliation with Rayona who forms a kind of family with Dayton and Christine. Mother and daughter go to bring Dayton's horse back from a stud farm. As this part of the novel finishes, their reconciliation is complete.

Part 3 is narrated by Ida, who finally reveals the secret that lies at the heart of the novel. In Ida's childhood, her mother, Annie, was sick and slowly dying. Annie's younger sister, the feckless Clara, comes to help the family in their time of need and is impregnated by Ida's undependable father, Lenco. Under pressure from the family to avoid a scandal, Ida agrees to go with Clara to Denver where she will have the baby secretly in a convent. Then Ida, as agreed, will claim the child as hers by another man.

The nuns at the convent believe the two young women are sisters. They coddle the pregnant Clara but treat Ida as little more than a servant. After Clara gives birth to her child, Christine, she refuses to return to the reservation. Ida returns instead with Christine, who everyone believes is her own child. She cares for her ailing mother and the baby for four years, until one day Clara shows up and wants to take Christine and sell her to a wealthy white couple. Ida refuses, and with the support of her mother and a local priest, sends Clara on her way.

Time passes. Ida's mother dies, and with her father gone and her sister Pauline married, she continues to live alone in the family home with Christine. Will Pretty Boy, a handsome youth Ida once idolized, returns from the Vietnam War horribly disfigured. Ida shows him love and kindness, and he moves in with her. When his face is reconstructed, Ida fears Will may stay with her only out of pity, and she drives him away. She does not tell him she is pregnant. The child she bears is Lee. Ida raises Lee and Christine with love and care. In the end, the trials all three women have endured come into full focus, as does their ability to survive and ultimately triumph.

Major Themes

A Yellow Raft in Blue Water is a novel marked with deep compassion and empathy. Through his three central characters, Dorris gives us a complete and multifaceted portrait of the struggles faced by Native American women in a society that is sexist, racist, and often uncaring. Principal themes include the victimization of native women, empowerment, alienation, and the redemptive power of love.

The Victimization of Native American Women

Each of the three Native American women in the novel falls victim to society's prejudices. One of the most extreme cases of victimization presented is Rayona's sexual molestation by the middle-aged priest Father Tom. Rayona is doubly a victim of society. As writer Janet St. Clair points out in her 1999 essay, "Fighting for Her Life: The Mixed-Blood Woman's Insistence Upon Selfhood," Rayona Taylor is "the only character in contemporary Native American fiction who is half Indian and half [black.]" Abandoned by her father, Elgin, and alienated from a mother, who is incapable of caring for anyone but herself, Rayona drifts through life with little direction, rejected and scorned as not a full or true Indian by the Native American boys she comes in contact with. Ironically, it is the working-class white couple, Sky and Evelyn, who show real concern and love for her and "adopt" her temporarily into their family.

Christine, Rayona's wayward mother, is abandoned by Elgin, who cannot even stay by her side when she is seriously ill in the hospital. The fact that, as a young woman, Christine willingly allows herself to be used by men does not alter the reality that such abuse is wrong. Ida, the family's matriarch, would seem to be the least sympathetic of the three women, treating Christine with contempt. It is only in the final section of the novel that we learn the reasons that Ida has treated her "daughter" so. Ida is the novel's ultimate victim. Her family betrays her, forcing her to be mother to a child that is not her own, in order to save the family's reputation. Left alone to raise Christine without the help of relatives or friends, she denies herself happiness with the veteran Will, realizing that his family despises her and will never accept her as his wife. For these reasons, she keeps her pregnancy a secret from Will and raises Lee by herself.

The Redemptive Power of Love

Despite the difficulties faced by the three protagonists, Dorris sees hope and promise in the love they find and share. The careless indifference and selfish cruelty of such characters as Father Tom, Clara, and Elgin are counterbalanced by the selfless love of Sky, Evelyn, and Dayton. It is Sky and Evelyn who take Rayona to the Indian rodeo where she reconnects with her heritage and her family and finds a measure of self-respect and confidence in her bronco ride. Dayton, also a victim of prejudice and intolerance, takes in and cares for the dying Christine with a selfless love that seeks no reward. He is the catalyst that brings about the final reconciliation between mother and daughter. This situation is paralleled in Ida's narrative when she takes in the disfigured Will and loves and cares for him. She sacrifices her own happiness with him to allow Will to get on with his life, raising his child without his knowledge. In the end, the bonds of kinship and familial love for each of these unique women are stronger than the power of hatred, misunderstanding, and prejudice.

The Broken Cord
Summary and Analysis

The subtitle of Michael Dorris's moving memoir is "a family's ongoing struggle with fetal alcohol syndrome." The book is about Dorris's adoption of a three-year-old Native American boy and his gradual realization that fetal alcohol syndrome (FAS) has irreparably damaged his son's mind and body. How Dorris comes to accept and deal with this sobering reality lies at the heart of the narrative.

Dorris's desire, as a 26-year-old graduate student and instructor in anthropology at Yale University, to became an "unmarried father" leads him to Pierre, South Dakota, where he adopts three-year-old Adam (whose real name is Abel), a child described to him as "mildly retarded." Dorris is given temporary custody of Adam for a year before the adoption becomes finalized. During this time, he begins to see that Adam's problems are anything but mild. One January day, Dorris finds the boy unconscious on the floor and rushes him to a hospital, where doctors are unable to diagnose the cause of his seizure. A second seizure occurs during a blizzard, and after being treated and released from the hospital once again, Adam is put on regular medication to control his seizures.

Meanwhile, Dorris's academic career blossoms. He is hired by prestigious Dartmouth College to start a Native American studies department. Part Indian himself, Dorris makes friends with Native American Beatrice Medicine, a visiting faculty member. Beatrice invites Dorris and Adam to a powwow on a reservation in South Dakota, where her mother lives. It is a special time for both father and son. The two are given Indian names in a special naming ceremony. Adam is named Wooded Mountain and Dorris Eagle Wing. The reservation's residents are impressed by his son and, for the first time, Dorris notes that it is Adam, not he, "who fits in."

A student examination at the day-care center Adam attends determines that he is learning disabled (LD), a judgment that Dorris refuses to accept. "I willed Adam to be fine," he writes, "and he wasn't." Trying to compete with the two-parent families of other children at the day-care center Adam attends, Dorris bakes an elaborate train cake for Adam's birthday party. All goes well until the next day, when parents complain that their children's urine is colored, as a result of the food coloring used in the cake's icing.

Anxious to prove his son normal, Dorris takes him to a psychologist in Boston for testing. The psychologist confirms the opinion of the day-care center, again asserting that Adam has a serious learning disability. Dorris refuses to accept this and continues to rationalize his son's problems.

In 1974, Dorris adopts a second Native American child, Sava, who has no developmental disabilities. He moves his family into a new home off campus. Soon after, he adopts a third Indian child, a 10-month-old girl named Madeleine.

Now a tenured associate professor, Dorris meets a former student, Louis Erdrich, at a Native American powwow. They fall in love and correspond regularly, while Dorris and his three children are in New Zealand on a grant-sponsored trip. After their return to New Hampshire in 1981, Michael and Louise marry. Life is good for the new couple. Their writing careers begin to take off. Erdrich's first novel, *Love Medicine*, is a resounding success. The couple has two natural children—daughters Persia and Pallas. By this time, Adam is in high school and struggling to survive both academically and socially. Under the advice of school administrators, Dorris and Erdrich place him into a more suitable vocational program.

On a field trip to South Dakota, Dorris sees other boys behaving like Adam and learns about fetal alcohol syndrome for the first time from the program director. Dorris realizes that Adam suffers from FAS, brought on by his mother's excessive consumption of alcohol during pregnancy. He becomes obsessed with the condition and learns everything he can about it, through reading and interviewing experts in the field. The more he learns, the more driven he is to become a crusader in the fight to end FAS and treat it. He begins, with Adam's consent, to write the book that becomes this memoir.

The struggle for his parents to accept Adam and the apathetic attitude toward life he expresses as a result of his condition reaches a climax when the couple return home from a night out to find the bathroom flooded. Adam had caused the problem and then, instead of trying to do something about it, simply went to bed. Dorris must face the grim realization that Adam may never be able to function on his own in the world.

Anxious to find productive work for Adam, Dorris helps him get a summer position on the maintenance crew at the Saint Gauden National Historic Site in New Hampshire. Adam is able to do his job but is only motivated to do so when his boss is watching him. When he reapplies for the same job the following summer, he is turned down.

In the spring of 1988, Adam moves to a group home with other young people 20 miles from his family. He works as a dishwasher in the restaurant of a bowling alley. On his 21st birthday, Dorris drives to pick Adam up for a birthday party and finds that his son has lost his job and is again suffering seizures regularly due to low doses of medication.

"A drowning man is not separated from the lust for air by a bridge of thought—he is one with it—," he writes at the book's end, "and my son, conceived and grown in an ethanol bath, lives each day in the act of drowning. For him there is no shore."

The last chapter of the book is written by Adam who tells his own story. It is a poignant ending to an emotionally charged story.

Major Themes

The Broken Cord, winner of the National Book Critics Circle Award, brought fetal alcohol syndrome into the public spotlight for the first time. Readers experienced the wide range of emotions that Dorris experienced as he raised Adam. The memoir is a cry for help and understanding as well as a sharp critique of Native American alcoholism, especially among women, and the seemingly uncaring medical establishment that too often reduces the victims of FAS to mere statistics. Tragically, Adam/Abel died several years after the publication of the book, when he was struck by a car while walking along a roadway.

Fetal Alcohol Syndrome and Alcoholism among Native American Women

Fetal alcohol syndrome is caused by alcohol transferred during pregnancy from a mother to her unborn baby's developing body and brain. The effects are devastating to a child and irreversible. Most women know better than to drink during pregnancy, but FAS is a continuing problem particularly among Native American women. According to Jeaneen Grey Eagle, director of a rehabilitation program at the Pine Ridge village in South Dakota, who Dorris befriends and interviews, 50 percent of the pregnant women and girls on the reservation drink regularly.

Dorris delves into the problem, devoting an entire chapter of his book to the history of Indian alcohol use and alcoholism and its present state. He even writes frankly about his own excessive drinking in his youth. One report he quotes calls alcohol abuse "the most severe and widespread health problem among Indians today." Incidents of terminal cirrhosis, the fatal results of a lifetime of excessive drinking, are more than four times higher among Native Americans than the general population. An alarming proportion of young Indian women who drink die at an early age. Alcohol, Dorris explains, "had wiped out my son's natural family." Adam's mother died of the effects of alcoholism at age 33 and his father, also a chronic alcoholic, was murdered.

The anger directed toward these women who carelessly and irresponsibly put their unborn children at risk is something Dorris initially shares with Grey Eagle and other experts in the field. She suggests that these women should be put in jail as criminals. Dorris confronts and helps resolve his anger through his book, which he says at one point evolved from "a footnoted study of the natural implication of fetal alcohol syndrome" into "the chronicle of a personal quest for understanding."

LESLIE MARMON SILKO

Biography

AN ACTIVIST AND WRITER of poetry, novels, and short stories, Leslie Marmon Silko is one of the leading Native American writers of her generation. She was born on March 5, 1948, in Albuquerque, New Mexico, the eldest of three daughters, and is of Laguna Pueblo, Mexican, and European ancestry. Her father, Lee Howard Marmon, was a photographer. As a child, Leslie Marmon listened to her grandmother and aunts telling her the stories of the Pueblo people, and it heavily influenced her later writing. Silko wrote her first short story in fifth grade, creating it out of assigned spelling words.

She attended Catholic school and then earned a B.A. from the University of New Mexico in 1969. That same year saw the publication of Silko's first short story, "The Man to Send Rain Clouds," in the *New Mexico Quarterly*. The story, which is still anthologized today, helped her earn a National Endowment for the Humanities Discovery Grant. It was also the year that her three-year marriage to Richard C. Chapman—which produced a son, Robert—ended in divorce. A second marriage to John Silko in 1971 produced a second child, Cozimir, and also ended in divorce.

Silko's early published stories and poems were collected in her first book, *Laguna Woman*, in 1974. Her first novel, *Ceremony* (1977), is about a Native American World War II veteran and his struggle for redemption through traditional Native American rituals. It is among the most critically praised of all Native American novels and is a staple in high school and college curricula. Her much-anticipated second novel, *Almanac of the Dead*, an ambitious historical novel, did not appear until 1991. The book met with mixed reactions from critics. Some of them took the writer to task for her seeming advocacy of a violent revolution and for taking an antigay stand. Her most recent novel, *Garden in the Dunes* (1999), is

63

about women's history, slavery, and other issues. Her short stories and poems are collected in the multigenre work *Storyteller* (1981). *Delicacy and Strength of Love*, her collected correspondence with fellow writer James Wright, appeared in 1986.

Silko has taught in New Mexico and Alaska and, since 1978, has been on the faculty of the University of Arizona in Tucson. In 1981, she was awarded a MacArthur Foundation "genius grant."

Silko's attacks in essays on other Native American writers, including Louise Erdrich and Gary Snyder, have focused on what she sees as their exploitation or abandonment of Native American traditions and values.

"You can look at the old stories [of Native American folklore] that were told among the tribal people here in a north country and see that within them is the same kind of valuable lessons about human behavior and that we need them still," she said in an interview.

Ceremony
Summary and Analysis

Ceremony is the story of Tayo, a mixed-blood Native American who returns from service in the Pacific in World War II deeply troubled and alienated. The psychological trauma he suffered as a prisoner of the Japanese lands Tayo in a veteran's hospital before he is released and allowed to return home to New Mexico and the Laguna Pueblo reservation. He lives with his Auntie, the mother of his dead cousin Rocky, and works on a sheep ranch with his friend and fellow soldier Harley. Harley and Leroy, another Native American ex-soldier, escape from the dark memories of wartime by getting drunk, picking up women, and boasting about their war experiences. Tayo has a deeper spiritual need and finds his friends' behavior fruitless and unfulfilling. His attempts to reconnect with his people's traditions are frustrated by his friends and his own psychological problems. He is burdened by a heavy guilt over a drought that grips the reservation and that he blames on his cursing the Japanese jungle rains. He also feels guilt over Rocky's death during the war, which he was unable to prevent. He is even haunted by his refusal to kill a Japanese soldier, who he believed was his Uncle Josiah.

Tayo's problems, however, began long before he went to war. His white father abandoned him and his mother soon after Tayo's birth. His mother, Laura, was an irresponsible parent who neglected him as a child while she drank and had sexual encounters with different men, sometimes for money. Tayo later was cared for by his grandmother and aunt who never let him forget the shame his mother brought to their family.

Things grow worse for Tayo when Emo, another Indian veteran, boasts about his life of killing in the war and taunts Tayo, calling him a half-breed. Tayo's anger erupts in violence, and he attacks Emo in a bar with a broken bottle. Fortunately, his friends stop him before he can kill Emo. Tayo is arrested and sent to an army psychiatric hospital in Los Angeles. A doctor who befriends him allows Tayo to return to the reservation. There, his grandmother sends him to Ku'oosh, the tribal medicine man, to be healed of his troubled soul. Ku'oosh performs a healing ceremony on Tayo, which eases his pain but does not remove it entirely. Ku'oosh realizes that Tayo will need something stronger to eradicate the devils that haunt him.

Ku'oosh sends Tayo to Betonie, a different kind of medicine man who, like Tayo, is of mixed heritage. Betonie, who lives in Gallup, New Mexico, is an expert at helping war veterans, but Tayo has little confidence that he can cure him. Everything about Betonie makes Tayo skeptical. His home is in a slum neighborhood, and the inside of his house is dirty and cluttered. With his assistant, Shush, also known as Bear, Betonie takes Tayo into the mountains for the healing ceremony. The medicine man's healing can only go so far, however. He tells Tayo that he must learn to heal himself from his deep and complex troubles. He tells him that a constellation of stars, a herd of spotted cattle, a woman, and a mountain will play important roles in his healing.

Back home, Tayo sees the reckless lives of his friends and is more appalled by their behavior than before. In a brawl over a white woman, Harley is badly beaten. Tayo is tired of their aimless existence and leaves for the mountains in search of his uncle's lost cattle. In the mountains he discovers a farm owned by a strange woman named Ts'eh Montano who takes him in. They become lovers. Ts'eh is both Tayo's lover and teacher. She guides him to find the constellation of stars Betonie referred to and helps him in his search for the lost cattle.

Tayo continues his search for the cattle and finds them behind a barbed wire fence. He cuts the fence to release them but is discovered by two cowboys on patrol for the rancher Floyd Lee, who has stolen the cattle. The cowboys begin to take Tayo back into town to have him arrested for rustling, but when they sight a mountain lion, they go off in pursuit of it and leave him behind. Tayo leaves with the cattle as snow begins to fall, covering the break in the fence and the trail of the cattle. He returns to Ts'eh who teaches him more about the ways of his people and warns him about Emo.

Emo, seeking revenge on Tayo, is spreading rumors that he has become mentally unstable again. Emo leads a posse to capture Tayo and send him back to the psychiatric hospital. Tayo flees and meets up with Harley and Leroy in their car. They take him for a drive, and Tayo falls asleep. When he awakens, he is alone in the car. Later, he sees Emo with Leroy and Pinkie, another Indian. They have tied Harley up in a truck and intend to kill him for allowing Tayo to go free. As Tayo watches in horror, they put Harley on a barbed wire fence. Armed with a screwdriver, Tayo is about to rush at Emo and kill him, but he resists the urge, realizing that violence is no answer to his troubles and will only make them worse. The others leave, and Tayo returns to his Auntie's house. He learns that Harley and Leroy have been found dead in the pickup truck after a horrendous accident. Pinkie is found dead, shot through the head. Emo and his evil live on, but Tayo has escaped him. He has completed the ceremony of his healing and is whole again. In a closing ritual poem, good triumphs over evil, but the reader is warned that the only way to maintain victory over evil is to be ever vigilant.

Major Themes

The richness of its themes is one reason why *Ceremony*, Silko's first novel, has become one of the most praised and read of all Native American novels. The fragmented narrative and the interspersed stories and legends made the book difficult for many readers on its publication in 1977, but over time, readers have adapted to Silko's style.

"When *Ceremony* first came out, it was considered to be really challenging, for the most sophisticated reader," Silko has said. "And then gradually, graduate students could read it, then juniors and seniors in college. . . . Now, precocious juniors in high school suddenly can read *Ceremony*."

The central story of one Native American's journey to stability and wholeness touches on many important themes common to Native American literature, including the sacredness of the land, the destructive power of collective and individual violence, the search for identity in a chaotic world, and the importance of ritual and ceremony in the process of healing.

Storytelling

Silko sees herself as part of a continuing line of storytellers in Native American tradition that for many generations was exclusively oral. She even titled her third book, a collection of various writings, *Storyteller.* "I had to discover for myself . . . ," she said in an interview in Germany, "that the old stories still have in their deepest level a content that can give the individual a possibility to understand."

The stories that intrude on the narrative in *Ceremony* are not meant as pleasant interludes or entertaining diversions. They relate directly to what is happening in the central story, commenting on and supporting the themes found there. A good example of this is the story of the Ck'o'yo gambler, Pa' caya' nyi. He told people that they did not have to take care of their cornfields, that he could do the work for them through magic. In saying this, Pa' caya' nyi was, in fact, tricking them. The corn crop failed, and the corn mother angel left the people's fields, which fell into ruin. The lesson taught by the story is that humans (including Tayo and his soldier friends) are easily led astray. By pursuing illusions and false promises, these young men fall out of favor with the natural world that is vital to the survival of the Pueblo people.

As Silko said in another interview in 1977, storytelling for Indians "is like a natural resource." Through hearing or reading these stories, the people learn about life and what values are important to growth and maturity. By the end of the novel, it is Tayo who tells his story of his encounters with the land and the mystical woman Ts'eh to the elders of the Pueblo. The story is taken as a sign of renewed life, not just for the storyteller but for all his people—a promise of good things to come.

The Importance of Place

Tayo's movement from a broken state to wholeness is a journey that occurs not just in time but in place too. The different landscapes he passes through, from the pueblo he calls home to Mount Taylor to the magical place where he finds and captures the spotted cattle, are filled with symbolic meaning. The "re-centering" that Tayo must accomplish to repair his shattered life is as much a geographical centering as a spiritual and mental one. He becomes fixed in places as much as the stars in the constellation Ku'oosh draws in the earth are fixed in the sky.

The healing power of place is dramatically enacted in the episode in which Tayo decides to take a walk after the bar closes. Leaving this place of confusion and distortion, he finds himself outside the pueblo near the adobe walls that were once the home of the woman known as the Night Swan, who he had a meaningful encounter with earlier. "In a world of crickets and wind and cottonwood trees he was almost alive again; he was visible. . . . The place felt good, he leaned back against the wall until its surface pushed against his backbone solidly."

Later, he meets another woman, the strange Ts'eh, who becomes his spiritual guide. She is closely identified with the land. At one point, Silko describes her body as a rich landscape where Tayo can be nurtured. When he tells about his encounter to the elders and Ku'oosh at the novel's end, they fully understand its significance. The story "re-establishes the Pueblo as the geographical (and hence spiritual) center of a visible world," writes Robert M. Nelson in his study *Place and Vision: The Function of Landscape in Native American Fiction,* "a particular landscape that contains, within itself, the power to heal and make whole and sustain life in the face of those destructive forces (both internal, and external to human consciousness) that cohabits the universe."

Storyteller
Summary and Analysis

Storyteller occupies a unique place in the writings of Leslie Marmon Silko. It is a multigenre work composed of eight short stories, retellings of traditional Pueblo tales and myths, poems, fragments of letter, vignettes of autobiography and family history, and twenty-six photographs that are interspersed throughout the text. The format and organization of the book make it like no other. There are no chapter headings, and the table of contents appears in the back of the book, not the front. Even its size sets *Storyteller* apart from other books, proportioned between a normal-sized novel and a large coffee table book. In content and structure, it is difficult to categorize.

All the stories and many of the poems in *Storyteller* have been previously published, but the careful arrangement and placement of them in the book among other writings give them a new and fresh perspective. The photographs of family members and friends among the Laguna people provide an important visual aid to the stories and other pieces.

While the stories—both Silko's original ones and the ones she retells—are written down, "frozen on the page," as she says, she has tried to re-create the sense of them being delivered orally by storytellers, of which she is only one of many. As the title indicates, the book is as much about the storytellers themselves as the stories they are telling.

The eight original stories range across different tribes and peoples—from the Navajo to the Hopi to a story about the historical Apache chief Geronimo. The most arresting story and the one that sets the pattern for the others is the title story, set in the frozen north of Alaska. "Storyteller" is about a Yupik girl who is in a jail cell awaiting interrogation concerning the death of a white storekeeper. In the course of the story, the young woman looks back over the events that brought her to the jail cell. Leaving her grandmother and her home village, she attended a government boarding school, where the teachers beat her when she spoke her native language instead of English. On returning to her village, she learns that her grandmother has died, and she goes to live with an old man who resided with her grandmother but is not her grandfather. He abuses her sexually. Adrift in a world she is trying to understand, the girl takes up with a young oil worker in the nearby oil fields, but he uses her solely for his own pleasures too. Along the way, she learns the truth behind the death of her parents years before. They were sold bad alcohol by an unscrupulous storekeeper and died of alcohol poisoning.

The old man, now confined to his bed, keeps repeating one story over and over. It concerns a hunter who is pursued across the frozen tundra by a bear. As the girl plots revenge for her parents' deaths, she identifies with the bear in the story. Using her sexuality as a tool, she lures a local storekeeper, who may or may not be the same man responsible for her parents' deaths, onto the frozen river. He falls through the ice and drowns.

A white, liberal lawyer who takes her case tries to get the girl to change her story of what happened, but she refuses. Her story is hers, she reasons, and to change it would be to tell a lie. "I intended that he die," she says. "The story must be told as it is." Like the old man, she ends up repeating the story over and over. "[S]he did not pause or hesitate," Silko writes, "she went on with the story, and she never stopped."

"A brooding fatalism hangs over this haunting fable of cruelty, misunderstanding, and revenge . . ." writes Helen Jaskoski in her book-length study of Silko's short fiction, "a disorienting instability of time and space contribute to the sense of myth."

The old Navajo woman Ayah in the second story in the collection, "Lullaby," has no story to comfort her other than the tale of her own miserable life. She stands outside a bar near the village of Cebolleta on a snowy evening, waiting for her husband, Chato, to return with some wine bought with their government check. When he finally returns, the old couple is caught in the snowstorm as they make their way home. To escape the storm, they climb a hill and find temporary shelter under some rocks. As these mundane events unfold, Ayah reviews the losses she has suffered. Two of her children died in infancy. Her eldest son, Jimmie, was killed in an unspecified war years earlier. Her only two remaining children, Danny and Ella, were taken away from her by the government to cure them of tuberculosis. When they returned years later for a visit, their mother was a stranger to them. They do not even speak the same language, having forgotten their native Navajo tongue. "It was worse than if they had died . . . ," Silko writes. "She [Ayah] carried the pain in her belly and it was fed by everything she saw."

Now in old age, Ayah does not even have the comfort of a loving marriage, having long been estranged from her husband. She faces her last loss—her own death in the snow—with a degree of understanding, acceptance, and peace.

Death is a regenerative act in "The Man to Send Rain Clouds," the most anthologized of all Silko's stories. It is the deceptively simple tale of the death of Teofilo, an old shepherd, whose body is discovered by his relatives under a large cottonwood tree. The community gathers and decides that, if they bury Teofilo with enough water to quench his thirst, he will return as part of the rain clouds that bring water and life to the pueblo.

In "Yellow Woman," another story that deals with myth and legend, a young wife and mother finds escape from her placid pueblo existence with a handsome stranger named Silva who whisks her away to his adobe hideaway atop a mountain. The narrator compares her experience to that of the legendary Yellow Woman who "went away with the spirit from the north." Whether Silva is a spirit or a real person is left for the reader to decide, but in the end the woman returns to her life in the pueblo, having found fulfillment, however briefly, with her mysterious lover.

The essence of native storytelling is succinctly captured in one of the legends that Silko retells in her book. In "Skeleton Fixer," a woman finds bones scattered across the ground. Old Man Badger carefully puts the bones together and from them emerges Old Coyote Woman who, once complete, runs off. Silko compares the bones to the words of a story that each time they are put together again and retold, come out a little differently. This difference lies in the art of the particular storyteller.

The sum of *Storyteller* is greater than its parts. The very act of storytelling is as important as the story itself. Silko seeks to lose herself in the generations of storytellers who precede and will follow her. The storyteller is a unifier, someone who brings the people together to share in the story's wisdom and be transformed by it. "Storytelling," she writes, "brings us together despite great distances between cultures, despite great distances in time."

Major Themes

In *Storyteller*, Silko attempted to create what she calls "a single form, a new thing which grows naturally out of [these] other forms of experience and expression." Through fragments, tales, myths, and photographs, she re-creates the world of the storyteller and his or her power to transform the world through narration and imagination. Storytelling for Silko is at the heart of the communal life she is a part of, both past and present.

Other themes that are explored in the collection are the struggle against colonialism and the subjugation of native peoples, the importance of language, and personal growth.

Superstition Versus Reason and Religion

The world of the Indians in Silko's stories is filled with magic and witchcraft. The most profound example is "Tony's Story," based on a real crime that took place in New Mexico in the early 1950s. In Silko's story, two friends, Tony and Leon, are together at the Feast of San Lorenzo (Saint Lawrence) in their pueblo. Leon has returned from military service and has been changed by living in the outside world of white men. Tony, who has remained in the pueblo, is bound by tradition and believes in the supernatural. During the festivities, the two encounter a white state police officer who, without reason, savagely attacks Leon. Leon is outraged by this injustice and takes his case to the tribal council, seeking justice. He warns that if the same racist officer attacks him again, he will kill him. Tony sees the attack in a different light. He believes the evil-minded cop is a witch and wears an amulet to protect himself from his power. He tries to get Leon to wear an amulet, but his friend refuses and scoffs at his superstitions.

Ironically, in a final confrontation with the malicious officer, it is Tony, the peace-loving one, who kills the policeman, while Leon looks on in shock. Tony, in a dream, saw the evil man as an obstacle to the coming of the much-needed rains on their land. "Don't worry, everything is O.K. now, Leon," Tony tells his friend after the killing. The last sentence of the story suggests that Tony may be right: " . . . in the west, rain clouds were gathering."

Whether the author believes in Tony's interpretation or not is left in doubt. There is less doubt in "The Man to Send Rain Clouds," in which the wise villagers thwart the Catholic priest Father Paul in his efforts to give the dead shepherd a Christian burial. The villagers not only get their way with the burial rite, they even enlist Father Paul in their plan. The priest is not depicted as a guiding light for the simple Pueblo people but a pathetic outsider who does not fit in with their community. The bonds of superstition and magic are strong and serve an important role in the native community, Silko seems to be saying.

Personal Empowerment Through Stories

In a story originally told to Silko by her Aunt Alice, a girl goes hunting and proves herself the equal of any boy or man. The story is set in a stretch of countryside known for its rock landmark. Every time a child passes the rock, he or she is re-minded by its elders of the story. Silko believes that such a story is meant to em-power every girl who hears it and that she also identified strongly with the girl in the story.

"People tell those stories about you and your family or about others and they begin to create your identity," the author said in an interview. The story, if mean-ingful, gives its teller strength to overcome adversity and, as in the case of the Yupik girl in "Storyteller," a defense against forces that would dominate and defeat her and her family. Even if the modern world rejects the story, the teller continues to stubbornly tell it, as the old man does in his bed.

As Elizabeth McHenry writes in an essay on Silko's book, "Blurring the boundaries between art and social science, she is able to introduce her readers to the fullness and fragmentation of her own private life and the life of Laguna culture."

In Silko's richly realized stories, the individual and the communal intertwine, informing and mutually supporting each other.

JOY
HARJO

Biography

A LEADING NATIVE AMERICAN POET whose poems depict the mythical past and often confusing present of the contemporary world, Joy Harjo was born on May 9, 1951, in Tulsa, Oklahoma, a member of the Muscogee (Creek) Nation, and grew up in New Mexico. Her aunt Lois Harjo Ball and her grandmother Naomi Harjo Foster were both painters. Harjo's father, a sheet-metal worker, left the family when she was young. She earned her B.A. from the University of New Mexico in 1976 and then earned a master of fine arts degree (M.F.A.) in creative writing at the University of Iowa in 1978. She published her first collection of poetry, *The Last Song*, in 1975. It was followed by the poetry collections *What Moon Drove Me to This?* (1979) and *She Had Some Horses* (1983). *Secrets from the Center of the World* (1989) was a unique collaboration with astronomer and photographer Stephen Strom that combined poems and photographs.

Harjo's fifth collection of poems, *In Mad Love and War* (1990), received the American Book Award and the Delmore Schwarz Memorial Award. She is also the recipient of the American Indian Distinguished Achievement in the Arts Award and the William Carlos Williams Award. Harjo has taught at several colleges including the Institute of American Indian Arts (1978–79), Arizona State University (1980–81), the University of Colorado (1985–88), the University of Arizona (1988–90) and the University of New Mexico, where she was a professor from 1991 to 1995. Her collected poems, *How We Became Human: New and Selected Poems 1975–2001*, appeared in 2002. Harjo has also written a children's book, *The Good Luck Cat* (2000), and several screenplays.

A poet with a strong social and political vision, Harjo has traveled widely, particularly to attend poetry festivals and spread goodwill to native peoples and

Latinos in Central America and elsewhere. She is also a professional musician and plays tenor saxophone with her band, Poetic Justice.

Harjo has won a Writer of the Year Award from the Wordcraft Circle of Native Writers and Storytellers three times, most recently in 2005 for her script for the film *A Thousand Roads*, made for and shown at the National Museum of the American Indian in Washington, D.C. She has also received the Lifetime Achievement Award from the Native Writers Circle of the Americas.

"I feel any writer serves many aspects of culture, including language," Harjo has said, "but you who serve history, you serve the mythic structure that you're part of, the people, the earth, and so on—and none of these are separate."

She Had Some Horses
Summary and Analysis

Harjo's third volume of poetry, *She Had Some Horses,* displayed a new maturity and growth in her work. Themes that are suggested in her earlier poems are more fully fleshed out and developed in this collection.

Harjo skillfully uses the rhythms and repetition of Native American chant and song in the title poem, which draws parallels between kinds of horses and different sides of the human personality. In doing so, Harjo draws on a rich tradition of horses as symbols of strength and beauty in Indian culture. "Horses, what the horses mean, a kind of love, brought together despite an opposition of culture, of place and time," she writes in the introduction to her collected poems. The horse plays an important role in her family history as well. The only artwork of her grandmother Naomi Harjo Foster not removed from the family's home by her father after he left following her parents' divorce was a charcoal drawing of two horses racing in a storm. Harjo dedicated *She Had Some Horses* to another family artist, her aunt Lois Harjo Ball.

According to Harjo, not all native women can necessarily paint or draw, but they possess an elemental creative force nonetheless. In the poem "For Alva Benson and for Those Who Have Learned to Speak," Harjo celebrates the act of giving birth, which she sees as connecting women to the earth itself:

> *And the ground spoke when she was born.*
> *Her mother did it. In Navajo she answered*
> *as she squatted down against the earth*
> *to give birth.*

The power of myth, however, does not drown out the grim reality of contemporary life for the Indian women Harjo writes about. Displaced and cut off from their traditional lives on reservations, many of these women are left adrift in large cities, where they are abused by men, often have numerous children to raise alone, and inhabit lives haunted by poverty and degradation. She describes Noni Daybright, the subject of the poem "Kansas City" as "a dishrag wrung out over bones." In "The Woman Hanging from the Thirteenth Floor," one of the most celebrated poems in this collection, a displaced native woman must decide if death is preferable to her unhappy and squalid life on the east side of Chicago. Women stand below and watch her standing on the precipice, realizing that they are "watching themselves." The pain that drove the woman to the brink of self-destruction is their pain too.

The woman who is the subject of the poem recognizes this fact as well:

> *She sees*
> *other buildings just like hers. She sees other*
> *women hanging from many-floored windows*
> *counting their lives in the palms of their hands*
> *and in the palms of their children's hands.*

The poem ends in ambiguity. The reader is left not knowing if the woman jumps or pulls herself back into her apartment and continues the struggle that her life has become.

One way some native women, and men, deal with the struggles they face in their lives is through alcohol use. In "Night Out," Harjo observes the insidious way that alcoholism destroys people looking to it for release and comfort. It is less a crutch, she is saying, than a trap for Native Americans:

> *You have to pay the cover charge thousands of times over*
> *with your lives*
> *and now you are afraid*
> *you can never get out.*

In another poem, "The Friday Before the Long Weekend," a teacher tries to instruct a drunken child, showing that each generation must deal with the curse of alcoholism. Harjo has written frankly about being in a relationship in her student days at the University of New Mexico with a man who drank "with such a vigor as if to kill himself." She has also confessed that "[s]ometimes I joined in the revelry in the bars or after hours and drank to obliterate the pain."

Major Themes

Despite the grim reality of life for many of her fellow native women, Harjo sees hope and promise through the language of poetry, tradition, and love. These are themes that reverberate throughout these poems.

The Power of Language to Transform

"I realize writing can help change the world," Harjo told Joseph Bruchac in an interview for his book *Survival This Way: Interviews with American Indian Poets*

(1987). "I'm aware of the power of language which isn't meaningless words. . . . Sound is an extension of all, and sound is spirit, motion."

The model for Harjo's cadence and rhythms in a number of her poems in this volume are the chants and drumbeats of native tribal ceremonial music. In "She Had Some Horses" and other poems the lines are chantlike, filled with repetitions that form a persistent litany. For the poet this repetition gives the reader "a way to enter in to what is being said and a way to emerge whole but changed." By reading her poems, Harjo imagines the reader absorbing the message and becoming empowered by her words. The point is made dramatically in "I Give You Back," a poem that attempts to exorcize the violence and injustice that has been done to native peoples over the centuries:

> *I am not afraid to be hungry.*
> *I am not afraid to be full.*
> *I am not afraid to be hated.*
> *I am not afraid to be loved.*

Through the strength of identity, Harjo is suggesting, lies the ultimate resistance to fear and abuse.

The Reassertion of Native Culture

While Harjo recognizes the way native cultures had been all but obliterated by European explorers, colonists, and the U.S. government in the past, she also believes these cultures have survived because of their richness and strength. In the poem "New Orleans," the poet revisits the history of the Creeks in the southeastern United States, people who were first introduced to white civilization by the expedition of Spanish conquistador Hernando de Soto in 1540. The voice of the Creeks is still there to be heard by those who listen:

> *There are voices buried in the Mississippi*
> *mud. There are ancestors and future children*
> *buried beneath the currents stirred up by*
> *pleasure boats going up and down.*

At one point, Harjo rewrites history and portrays the Creeks drowning de Soto in the river, even though in reality he died of fever and was buried by his own men. Later in the poem, Harjo claims that she saw de Soto

> *Having a drink on Bourbon Street*
> *Mad and crazy*
> *Dancing with a woman as gold*
> *As the river bottom.*

It is the land and its people that have proved to be the true treasures of North America, not the gold that de Soto and other Spanish explorers looked for in vain. The dance with the native woman also points to the assimilation and intermarriage that occurred, especially in Latin America, between Spanish settlers and the native population. Harjo's interest in the indigenous peoples of Latin America has brought her to visit many of these countries to read her work and participate in poetry festivals.

In Mad Love and War
Summary and Analysis

In Mad Love and War is Joy Harjo's fourth book of poems and her most commonly read and best-known volume. In it, she advances her poetic project and expands her vision as a writer. "The itinerary now sets out from survival," writes Laura Coltelli, "and leads into growth, from bearing history to history into active participation, from identification of distance to the striving to obliterate the gap."

The book is divided into two main sections, "The Wars" and "Mad Love." The first poem, "Grace," precedes the first section and serves as a preface. In it, Harjo compares the idea of grace to "a woman with time on her hands" or "a white buffalo escaping from memory." The poem looks forward to a spring that "was lean and hungry with the hope of children and corn." The poem is an appropriate preface, for transformation is one of the collection's central preoccupations. In one poem titled "Transformations," Harjo calls for a shift from hatred to love.

Before love can redeem humanity, however, the poet first takes a clear look at the contemporary world as it exists with all its ills—racism, violence, and the various conflicts that have colored modern history. The realities portrayed range from an inmate riot in a West Virginia prison depicted in "Legacy" to rebellion in a Nicaraguan town in "Resurrection."

"Strange Fruit," a dramatic monologue, is, like many of the poems, written in prose. It takes its title from the Lewis Allen song about lynching in the South, made popular by singer Billie Holiday. The poem is dedicated to National Association for the Advancement of Colored People (NAACP) organizer Jacqueline Peters, who was lynched by Ku Klux Klan members in Lafayette, California, in 1986. At the time, Peters was organizing support in opposition to the lynching the previous year of a 23-year-old black man. In the poem, Harjo imagines Peters speaking from beyond the grave to her murderers. "Please. Go away, hooded ghost from hell on earth. I only want heaven in my baby's arms, my baby's arms. . . . My feet betray me, dance away from this killing tree."

"For Anna Mae Pictou Aquash, Whose Spirit Is Present Here and in the Dappled Stars (for we remember the story and must tell it again so we may all live)" is addressed to Micmac activist Aquash, whose February 1976 murder at the Pine Ridge Reservation in South Dakota was as comparatively shocking as Peters's death. Aquash's murder is made all the more terrible, however, because it was covered up. Originally unidentified, Aquash's body was buried and later exhumed for a second autopsy, which revealed that she did not die of exposure as previously thought but from a bullet wound fired at close range into the back of her head. The crime was never solved.

In another poem, "We Must Call a Meeting," the poet turns to her ancestors and her rich heritage for answers to life's conflicts and injustices but finds no easy way to access them. "I am lost; I am looking for you," she writes. "Give me back my language and build a house / Inside it."

The last poem in this section, "The Real Revolution Is Love," sets the scene for the next section. In "Mad Love," human love and nature are powerful forces that redeem and transform. In "Crystal Lake," Harjo recalls childhood memories of fishing with her grandfather, a living link to the past. The past lives and renews the present in a poem like "Bleed Through," in which Harjo reconnects with her traditions and myths: "You are not behind a smoking mirror, but inside a ceremony of builders that has survived your many deaths." Love for another person is the subject of "Desire," "Healing Animal," and "Heartshed," in which the act of love is seen as another example of war.

With *In Mad Love and War,* writes Norma C. Wilson, Harjo "begins to emphasize not just overcoming fear through resistance but healing one's psychological wounds through love."

Major Themes

While many of the poems in *In Mad Love and War* are set in the contemporary world, they also hark back to Native American myth and traditions, a major theme in Harjo's poetry. The traditional folklore figure of the Trickster, usually a rabbit, recurs several times in these poems. Animals hold a significance for the poet based on their central role in Native American myths. The circle made by a flying eagle in "Eagle Poem" is like life itself "a true circle of motion," continually repeating itself. In "Nine Lives," a cat fights for one of its lives and "In the morning the winner will be grinning at the door of my sleep." Other themes that reverberate in the poems are nature as healer, the power of love to change the world and the self, and the never-ending struggle against injustice.

The Cleansing Power of Fire

As a literary symbol, fire is sometimes represented as a force of destruction, but for Harjo it is a cleansing force that destroys the bad and allows the good to rise up from its ashes. In the poem "City of Fire," she writes "We will . . . flood this city . . . with fire / with a revolutionary fire."

Fire is also equated with the creativity inside us all. It brings forth ideas and inspiration. "I have built a fire in the cave of my body," Harjo says in "Day of the Dead," "and hope the devil wind will give it a chance." In "We Must Call a Meeting," she identifies the artist's gift with the fire that shapes a pot in a kiln. "I am fragile," she says, "a piece of pottery smoked from fire / made of dung. . . ." The elements of fire and earth, as represented by the dung, are primeval and essential to her native culture's life and growth.

The Power of Music

A professional musician with her own band, Poetic Justice, it is not surprising that the lyricism and musicality of words play a central role in Harjo's poetry. Music is prominently featured in many of the poems in *In Mad Love and War*. It is a creative force, an expression of love, and a link to her Indian heritage. The woman dancer in the bar in "Deer Dancer" transcends her tawdry environment through the music and her response to it.

While the traditional dance and music of her native people is important to Harjo, it is modern jazz, a more urban and modern genre, that seems to fascinate her most. "The language of jazz kept me up at night or woke me up early in the morning [during the mid-eighties] as I wrote in the manner of the horn riffs that carried me over the battlefield," she writes in the introduction to her collected poems. " . . . [P]oetry and music have been together since the invention of poetry and music. They are soul mates, not meant to be parted."

"Strange Fruit" recalls the song that jazz singer Billie Holiday made famous, while "Rainy Night" is dedicated to Holiday. Harjo, recalling the challenges she has faced, identifies with Holiday, a drug addict at the end of her tragic life. "We would hold you closer than / the pain / you felt you deserved," she writes, addressing the singer.

"Bird" is a tribute to another jazz legend, Charlie Parker, who, like Harjo, played the tenor saxophone. In "Healing Animal," she refers to jazz musician John Coltrane, whose compositions were filled with a striving for spiritual love. Still, music for Harjo is equally identified with earthly love and eroticism. She speaks of "love in the fluid shape of a saxophone" in "Healing Animal" and in "Original Memory" compares making music to making love. The power of music to reinvent life and love is central to "We Encounter Nat King Cole as We Invent the Future." Here, the poet listens to the great African-American pop singer, who was also an accomplished jazz pianist, as she talks about old loves and broken-off affairs with a friend.

In the final analysis, music unites people, fusing them into a community, whether it be one in today's world or a community built on the heritage of the past. In "Healing Animal," Harjo describes the transcending power of music as it "climbed out of his [a musician's] trombone into the collected heartbeat of his tribe."

LOUISE ERDRICH

Biography

THE MOST PROLIFIC and arguably most prominent of Native American women novelists, Louise Erdrich has often employed multiple narrators in her novels to create powerful, layered portraits of reservation and small town life, past and present.

She was born Karen Louise Erdrich on June 7, 1954, in Little Falls, Minnesota, the eldest of seven children. Her father is of German descent and her mother French and Ojibwe. Her grandfather was tribal chairman for the Turtle Mountain Band of Chippewa. Louise grew up in Wakpeton, North Dakota, where her parents taught at the Bureau of Indian Affairs (BIA).

Erdrich attended Dartmouth College in 1972, where she studied under her future husband Michael Dorris. After graduating with a B.A. in English, she worked at a variety of jobs including lifeguard, construction flagwoman, and a teacher of poetry in prisons. She earned a master of fine arts (M.F.A.) degree in creative writing from Johns Hopkins University in 1979 and began to publish poems and short stories. She became reacquainted with Dorris, and the couple married in 1981. Her story "The World's Greatest Fisherman" was awarded the Nelson Algren Prize for short fiction in 1982. Her first novel, *Love Medicine*, appeared in 1984 and was awarded the National Book Critics Circle Award. The highly praised novel about two interconnecting reservation families has remained in print since its publication and was revised and expanded by the author in 1993. More novels followed, including *Tracks* (1988), about a trickster figure in nineteenth-century Native American culture, and *The Crown of Columbus* (1991), her only acknowledged collaborative novel written with Dorris.

After their adoptive son Jeffrey Sava accused the couple of child abuse, Erdrich and Dorris separated in 1995 and later began divorce proceedings. Dorris committed suicide in 1997. Erdrich's first published novel after his death, *The Antelope Wife* (1998), was also her first book with a nonreservation setting. Other works include *Baptism of Desire: Poems* (1990), the autobiographical *The Blue Jay's Dance: A Birthyear* (1995), and *The Game of Silence* (2005), her fourth children's book. Erdrich's most recent novel, *The Plague of Doves* (2008), has garnered some of her best reviews since *Love Medicine*. In a review in the *New York Times*, Michiko Kakutani called it "arguably her most ambitious—and in many ways, her most deeply affecting—work yet."

In April 2007, Erdrich refused an honorary doctorate from the University of North Dakota over her opposition to the school's Indian mascot, the Fighting Sioux. She lives in Minneapolis, Minnesota, with her three youngest children, where she owns and operates a bookstore, Birchbark Books, and Birchbark Press, an Ojibwe-language publishing company.

"[My writing style] is a mixture of the Ojibwe storyteller and the German system-maker," she said in one interview. "I feel that everything that I write has to be connected into this grand scheme."

Love Medicine
Summary and Analysis

Erdrich's first novel, *Love Medicine*, is primarily set on an Ojibwe reservation bordering the fictitious town of Pluto, North Dakota. Its intersecting short narratives chronicle the lives of five Native American families over five decades. Many of the characters from the novel reappear in her subsequent four North Dakota novels and form a mythical community that has been compared in scope and range to the fictional Yoknapatawpha County in Mississippi created by novelist William Faulkner in his novels and stories. In 1993, Erdrich reissued a new, expanded edition of her novel that includes several new chapters and places the novel more firmly in the cycle of her other books.

The novel begins with a central character who never again appears in person but haunts the other members of her extended family like a troubling ghost. During Easter weekend 1981, June Kashpaw is planning to take a bus home to the reservation she left years before. Her plans take a detour when she meets a blue-collar white man in a bar. They drive out to the country in the man's car and make love. When he falls asleep, June gets out and begins to walk home in a snowstorm and perishes.

After June's death, family members gather at the home of her sister, Zelda. They include Zelda's daughter, Albertine Johnson, the narrator of this sequence; her cousin Lipsha; and June's son King and his white wife, Lynette. One of a number of characters who feels estranged from the reservation, which was once his home, King's anger explodes while drinking, and he nearly drowns his wife in a vicious struggle. The violence affects the other family members when King and Lynette smash the pies the women had baked for the occasion.

The novel flashes back to 1934 and tells the story of Marie Lazarre, the family matriarch. As a young girl, Marie feels a religious calling and goes to a neighboring convent to become a nun. However, a fateful meeting with Nector Kashpaw changes both their lives. Nector has returned to the reservation to marry his first love, Lulu Nanapush, but is immediately and hopelessly attracted to Marie. "I don't want her, but I want her," he says, "and I can't let go." Although he ends up marrying Marie, Nector is still drawn to Lulu and ends up sharing his life with both women.

Lulu marries Henry Lamartine, who later dies, and has eight sons with several different men. In an episode set in 1957, Beverly Lamartine, the childless brother of Henry, visits Lulu with the intention of taking Henry Jr. away to raise as his own. Instead Beverly is seduced by Lulu and, like Nector, becomes a man with two women. This same year, Nector leaves Marie for Lulu but will later return to Marie.

The narrative shifts back to Albertine, who in 1973 runs away from home and arrives by bus in Fargo, North Dakota. There she accidentally meets Henry Lamartine Jr., who is returning from military service in the Vietnam War. They check in to a motel room, where it becomes clear that Henry's war experience has left him deeply troubled. The following year, Henry kills himself, and his cousin Lyman symbolically sinks Henry's prized red convertible, which the two had once driven to Alaska, into a river.

Next we meet another troubled son of Lulu, Gerry Nanapush, who has spent much of his adult life in and out of prison. Gerry keeps breaking out of jail to be with his wife, Dot Alore, but when he kills a state trooper, he is sentenced to life in prison, and Dot is left to raise their baby daughter alone.

Returning to 1981, we meet Gordie, June's former husband, who is racked by guilt at her death and gets drunk. Driving home, he hits a deer and loads it into his car, thinking he can sell the meat. But the deer is only stunned and revives in the car. Believing the animal is possessed by June's spirit, Gordie beats the deer to death with a crowbar. Then he drives to the convent and confesses to a bewildered nun that he has killed his wife. He flees and later is arrested by the tribal police.

Lipsha Morrissey wants to help reconcile his grandfather Nector with his grandmother Marie. He decides to give her "love medicine," raw turkey heart, to feed Nector and break the spell that Lulu still holds over him. In an ironic turn, Nector chokes on the turkey heart and dies, his ghost returning to haunt both Lipsha and Marie. Lulu, now old and nearly blind, also sees Nector's ghost. Marie makes her peace with her longtime rival and takes care of Lulu after she undergoes an eye operation.

The last scene of this complex narrative takes place in 1984. Lipsha visits King and Lynette, hoping to learn about Gerry, his father. As they play cards, a report comes on television that Gerry has once more escaped from prison. Suddenly, Gerry enters the house and accuses King of betraying him while in prison. The men play cards for King's car, bought with the insurance money from June's death. Lipsha wins the game. The police break in to recapture Gerry, but he escapes. Later, driving King's car, Lipsha discovers his father hiding in the trunk. Father and son reconnect and exchange stories as they drive. Lipsha takes his father to the Canadian border and freedom and then returns home, feeling free and whole.

Major Themes

The major themes that permeate Erdrich's novel are echoed time and again in later books in the series, as characters reappear earlier and later in their lives. *Love Medicine* weaves a complicated pattern as the stories, told by six different characters and an omniscient narrator, circle around one another. Although seemingly unrelated, the stories gradually come together to form the community that the twenty main characters inhabit. "[I]n the light of enormous loss, they [Native American writers] must tell the stories of contemporary survivors while protecting and celebrating the cores of cultures left in the wake of the catastrophe," Erdrich has written. Major themes in the novel include survival, renewal of the land, and the importance of community.

Love's Power

Although living in a grim contemporary reality, Erdrich's characters are immersed at the same time in a world of their ancestors—a realm of dreams, ghosts and spirits, and magic. In the novel, falling in love is most often portrayed not as a conscious decision but as something over which the individual has no control. The idea of love as a magical bewitching experience is most dramatically seen in the central triangle of Nector, Marie, and Lulu. Nector's memorable first encounter with Marie on the hill by the convent starts as a physical fight and ends in a sexual experience. Nector is immediately pulled into Marie's sphere of influence, unable to tear himself away from her. Lulu, who he was planning to propose to, is temporarily forgotten. Marie dominates Nector in their long marriage and makes him into something more than he otherwise would have been. When he visits Lulu later, however, he is again bewitched and ends up living with her for five years. The "love medicine" that Lipsha concocts to stop Nector from returning to Lulu can only kill him. For Erdrich, there is no cure for the witchery of love; the only way out of its web for Nector is death.

Beverly's marriage to Lulu is shown as similarly magical. He comes to take Henry Jr. away and ends up marrying Lulu and becoming a bigamist. Less life affirming is the relationship of King to his white wife, Lynette. They nearly kill each other in a savage struggle that stands in stark contrast to Nector and Marie's more playful tussle. For the most part, however, Erdrich depicts her bewildered lovers with humanity, warmth, and humor.

The Quest for Home

The need to return home is a driving force for many of Erdrich's characters. June, in the novel's opening chapter, perishes attempting to walk home in an Easter snowstorm. Her unfinished journey is mirrored in the final scene when Lipsha, having reconnected with his father, drives the car bought with June's insurance money across a bridge and homeward to the reservation. "Crossing the Water" is the title of this chapter, and the act of crossing water emerges as a potent symbol throughout the novel. Earlier, Lulu crosses water in a boat to reach the home of her first lover, Moses Pillager, who lives on an island.

For some characters, though, coming home is an unhappy event. King, who lives in the city of Minneapolis, finds himself frustrated and angry when he returns to the reservation to memorialize his dead mother. For those characters who find a way to deal with the struggles and confusion in their lives, coming home is a goal that brings the promise of a brighter future.

A Plague of Doves
Summary and Analysis

In this, her most recent novel, Erdrich returns to the tiny town of Pluto, North Dakota, the setting of *Love Medicine* and a number of her other novels. As in much of her earlier fiction, she employs multiple narrators to tell a tangled tale of a crime committed long ago, its shattering aftermath, and the long-term effects it has on a number of characters whose lives are intertwined.

The first section is narrated by Evelina Harp, a precocious young girl who is part white and part Ojibwe. A romantic who is always falling in love, Evelina is particularly taken by Corwin Peace, who is also part Indian. Evelina adores her Indian grandfather Mooshum, a colorful character who is the repository of the family and tribal history. It is Mooshum who tells Evelina about the title plague that struck the town back in 1896. The doves were actually passenger pigeons, a bird that later became extinct from being overhunted. The bird emerges as a symbol for Pluto itself, which another character later claims "is dying."

Evelina attends a Catholic school where she is taught by Sister Mary Anita, a mannish nun the students make fun of. Evelina comes to empathize with Sister Mary and develops a deep affection for her. When Mooshum identifies Sister Mary as a member of the Buckendorf family, a prominent German-American clan, he tells his granddaughter that the Buckendorfs were responsible for the hanging of three of his friends. He proceeds to tell the dark tale of how he, Cuthbert, Asiginok, and his nephew Holy Track came upon the bodies of five members of a murdered white farm family on the edge of town decades earlier. Miraculously, an infant child survived the massacre. When the Buckendorfs and other whites came upon the scene, they immediately believed the Indians were the murderers.

Without benefit of trial, the four are taken off to be hanged. Mooshum is cut down from the hanging tree before he dies, supposedly because he was related by marriage to one of the white families.

In the next section, the narrative shifts to Judge Antone Bazil Coutts, who is part Chippewa. He recalls another scandal in Pluto's more recent past, when the respectable banker John Wildstrand ran off with his young lover, the full-blooded Indian Maggie Peace. Their story begins when Maggie's young brother, Billy, abducts Wildstrand at gunpoint to pressure him to help support Maggie, who is pregnant with his child. In one of the novel's most humorous passages, Wildstrand convinces Billy to let him go and abduct his wife, Neve, instead. With the ransom money Wildstrand will pay Billy, he can be sure that Maggie is well taken care of. Neve will never suspect that the money is going to her husband's lover.

The plot works, but the kidnapping changes Neve from an indifferent wife to a passionate woman. Wildstrand later leaves her and goes off to live with Maggie and their newborn child, who will grow up to be Corwin Peace. Wildstrand goes back to his house and confronts Neve. They fall into each other's arms, but all is not forgiven when Wildstrand confesses his involvement in the kidnapping to Neve. She reports him to the police, and Wildstrand goes to prison.

The next part of the novel is narrated by another young, impressionable girl, 16-year-old Marn Wolde. She meets Billy, who has returned from army service in the Korean War, and is now a charismatic preacher. Billy captivates Marn's heart, and they marry and have two children. The couple later moves back to Marn's farm with her parents. Billy's power over his followers becomes stronger and stronger, and he founds a cult. As cult leader, he has sexual relations with other women. Marn is devastated but finds solace in her own fanaticism, snake handling, which is mentioned in the Bible. Overcome with anger at Billy and his evil ways, Marn murders him with snake venom.

The next section briefly returns to Evelina, who is working as a waitress in a luncheonette. Marn comes in for a meal with her children, and she asks Mooshum and Evelina to tell Judge Coutts that she wants to see him, undoubtedly about Billy's death.

The narrative again returns to the judge, who suspects Corwin has stolen the precious violin belonging to Shamengwa, Mooshum's brother. Corwin has indeed stolen the master musician's instrument but is unable to sell it. He is caught while pretending to play the violin on the street. Judge Coutts sees potential in Corwin and sentences him to report to Shamengwa every day to take violin lessons. Corwin dutifully does so and gradually becomes a master of the violin. Shamengwa dies, and Corwin plays the violin at his funeral. He shocks everyone when he then smashes the instrument against the coffin and drops its remnants inside. The judge picks up a letter that fell from inside the violin. Its contents reveal that the violin was fashioned from a canoe by the Peace brothers, Corwin's ancestors, and was intended for him all along.

The narrative returns to Evelina who, in 1972, is going off to college. An avid reader, she has discovered the diaries of Anaïs Nin and becomes obsessed by the writer who describes her numerous affairs with men and women in her voluminous writings. Evelina gets a job during the summer as a psychiatric aide at a state mental hospital. There she meets a new patient, Nonette, a troubled but beautiful girl who was molested at an early age by her cousin. Nonette seduces Evelina, who surprisingly finds herself attracted to Nonette, and the two end up in bed together. The next day, Nonette announces that she is leaving the hospital with her parents. Evelina is stunned. No sooner does she discover her love for Nonette than she loses her. She sinks into a deep depression and unexpectedly finds herself a patient in the same ward where she had previously worked. Corwin comes to visit her and plays his new violin for her. The music spells freedom for her and, with a little encouragement from Corwin, she leaves the hospital with him and returns to Pluto.

Evelina visits her old friend Sister Mary Anita. She now understands why she was so attracted to her. Sister Mary reveals to her former student that many years earlier Mooshum betrayed the other Indians by testifying against them before the white mob. This is the real reason why he was spared death. Evelina confronts her grandfather with this information, and he admits his guilt. He takes Holy Track's boots out to the tree from which the three men were hanged many years before and throws the boots over a branch in his memory.

Corwin, who has never abandoned Evelina, asks her to marry him, despite her sexual confusion. They seem to have been destined for each other from the beginning of this tangled story. The section ends with a joyous occasion—the marriage of Judge Coutts to Geraldine, Shamengwa's niece.

The next section is narrated by Judge Coutts. On the night of his marriage to Geraldine, he recalls the other great love of his life, an older woman, the town doctor, who he refers to only as C. Their passionate affair is conducted in secret, as the maturing Coutts works as a gravedigger in the town cemetery and eventually becomes its manager. Believing the difference in their ages is too great to overcome, C marries another man, the ruthless developer Ted Bursap, who buys old houses and tears them down to erect cheap, ugly new buildings in their place. Coutts is devastated. After a year, the two cannot resist their former attraction and resume their affair. Coutts, who has lived all his life with his mother, begins to study law and eventually becomes a judge. Meanwhile, his mother's health begins to fail, and he moves her into a convalescent home. He decides to sell their old house, but Ted Bursap is the only one to meet his price. Coutts decides that he would rather give up the house than his relationship with C and agrees to sell it to "the tear down king."

While Bursap is starting to demolish the old house, Coutts goes to C and asks her to run away with him, leaving everything behind. Instead, learning what Bursap is doing, she goes to the house and tries to stop him; but he is determined to tear down the house, realizing that his wife is Coutts's lover. As he knocks down a wall, a huge beehive is opened, and the bees repeatedly sting both Bursap and C. Both survive, but Bursap dies a year later. C breaks off her relationship with Coutts, and they meet briefly years later when she is an old woman.

Returning to the present, the judge learns from Geraldine that his lover, whose name is revealed to be Cordelia, refused to treat Indians. Coutts, she says, was the one "exception." We also learn Cordelia's identity and her reason for hating Indians: She was the child who survived the murders all those years before.

The closing section of the novel is narrated by Doctor Cordelia Lochren. Now an old woman, she spends her retirement running the local historical society, musing over the slow death of Pluto, and taking long walks with her dear friend Neve.

As the town historian, she plays an important role in the dying community. "I became the repository of many untold stories such as people will finally tell when they know there is no use in keeping secrets," she says. One secret exposed long before is that the distraught boyfriend of the murdered family's older sister was the actual killer. The boy, Tobeck Hess, disappeared after the murders and fled to Canada, where he joined the military, serving and dying in World War I. But twenty years before, Cordelia learned that Tobeck was as innocent of the murders as the three Indians who were hanged. She treats the wound of a cranky farmer, Marn's father, Warren Wolde, who is distraught at meeting her. Years later, he dies and leaves money to Cordelia in his will. She realizes that it was guilt over the murders that drove him to give her the money. "My last act as the president of Pluto's historical society," she says in the book's final page, " is this: I would like to declare a town holiday to commemorate the year I saved the life of my family's murderer." In forgiveness, Cordelia has found the peace that has eluded her much of her life.

Major Themes

All of Erdrich's Pluto novels deal with people, both Indian and non-Indian, struggling to find meaning in their lives through relationships set against the backdrop of a community in flux. In *The Plague of Doves*, that community seems on the verge of extinction, as young people move away to find new lives and opportunities and the old die, taking the lessons of the past with them. It is up to the individual to take a stand and grasp meaning and happiness, as Judge Coutts notes as he reviews his life: "[M]y work in the cemetery told me every day what happens when you let an unsatisfactory present go on long enough: it becomes your entire history."

History, both joyous and tragic, haunts many of Pluto's residents, but they carry on, as Mooshum does, with stoicism and good humor. It is Cordelia, however, the sole survivor of that terrible crime, who has the last word in the novel. It is her humanity and understanding that ends the novel on an affirmative note.

Intolerance and Injustice

"Solo," the chilling prologue to the novel, depicts the unnamed killer of Cordelia's family about to murder the last member of the family left alive, an infant in her crib. The killer's gun jams on the last bullet, and he puts a record on the family gramophone as he methodically repairs it, while the infant looks on. The reader learns much later in the novel that he spares the child.

As horrible as this opening scenario is, even more terrible is the lynching of the three Indians falsely accused of the killings. The murders were the rash work of a single madman, the lynchings committed in cold blood by a group of otherwise rational white men, some of them among Pluto's most upstanding citizens. The Indians, treated as second-class citizens, are summarily executed without benefit of trial. This act of "rough justice" echoes through the years and affects the lives of both those guilty and innocent and their descendants.

The racial intolerance that leads to the murders is paralleled by the religious intolerance of Billy Peace, the Indian who becomes an itinerant preacher. Billy uses his gifts of oratory to draw followers and then betrays them, setting himself up as a kind of god, one who preys on the women in his cult. Billy, in an ironic turn, is ultimately destroyed by his own fanaticism. Marn, his longsuffering wife and perhaps the book's most compelling narrator, turns into a snake-handling fanatic and kills her husband with venom. Erdrich draws on the biblical symbolism of the Garden of Eden as she describes Billy's demise: "I took the needle filled with the venom of the snake and tipped with the apple of good and evil. . . . Then I pushed the needle quickly, gently, like an expert, for I'd seen this many times in my pictures, right into the loud muscle of his heart."

Forgiveness and Redemption

Cordelia's ultimate act of forgiving the man who killed her family frees her from a burden of hatred, just as her long love affair with Antone Bazil Coutts, who is partially of Native American heritage, atones for her aversion to the Indians she initially believed were the murderers.

Sister Anita Mary, whose family members were among the lynchers of the Indians, redeems their sins by becoming a teacher and a nun and has a powerful influence on Evelina, one of the novel's pivotal characters.

Corwin Peace, the wayward son of Maggie and John Wildstrand, finds forgiveness, not "rough justice" at the hands of Judge Coutts. Instead of sending Corwin to prison for the theft of Shamengwa's precious violin, he sentences him to learn to play the instrument. Shamengwa becomes Corwin's mentor and through music puts him in touch with his tribal heritage. Music and its power save Corwin from a life of crime, and through his music he moves others, including the patients at the state mental hospital and the mourners at Shamengwa's funeral. More importantly, Corwin's music frees Evelina from her deep depression over her failed relationship with Nonette and helps her return to a new life in her community.

In contrast, Ted Bursap, Cordelia's cold-hearted husband and the destroyer of Pluto's past, cannot forgive Coutts for his relationship with his wife. In the vengeful act of tearing down Coutts's family homestead, Bursap is stung by the bees released from the house. While he survives this assault, Coutts tells us he dies a year later from a single sting of a bee, an insect that comes to symbolize the harmonious natural world that is so closely bound to the Native American past.

RIGOBERTA MENCHÚ

Biography

RIGOBERTA MENCHÚ won the 1992 Nobel Peace Prize, in recognition, in the words of the Nobel Committee, "of her work for social justice and ethno-cultural reconciliation based on respect for the rights of indigenous peoples." A large part of her efforts was focused on drawing the world's attention to the plight of the people of her native Guatemala during a 30-year civil war.

She was born Rigoberta Menchú Tum on January 9, 1959, in Laj Chimel, a village in Quiche province, Guatemala. Her family is descended from the native people who once inhabited the region, the Maya. Vicente Menchú, her father, was a community leader who worked with Peace Corps volunteers from the United States. The turbulent civil war between government forces and communist guerrillas that engulfed the country soon after Rigoberta's birth would eventually permanently alter her life. Like many villages, Chimel was visited by guerrillas, which resulted in the community becoming the focus and target of government troops. Over a period of years, both of Menchú's parents, two of her brothers, her sister-in-law, and three nieces and nephews were tortured and killed by government troops or agents. Their deaths led Menchú and several other relatives to become ardent antigovernment activists. She fled her homeland at age 20 and moved to Mexico, where she worked with other Guatemalans in exile to spread word of the atrocities back home.

In 1982, Menchú was interviewed extensively about her life and work by Venezuelan-French anthropologist Elizabeth Burgos. The interviews were collected in a book titled *My Name is Rigoberta Menchú and this is how my conscience was born.* The book became a best-seller and was translated into English under the title *I, Rigoberta Menchú.*

That same year, Menchú moved to Geneva, Switzerland, to work for the United Nations (UN). For the next twelve years, she helped establish the Work Group, an organization of indigenous peoples from around the globe. After winning the Nobel Prize, Menchú returned to Guatemala, where she was greeted as a hero by many of her country's citizens and as a troublemaker by the government. The long civil war ended in 1996, and in 1997 Menchú filed complaints in a Spanish court to press criminal charges against the Guatemalan government that had previously been in power. She knew she would not find justice in Guatemalan courts, because many judges were themselves implicated in political crimes. On December 23, 2006, after years of government bureaucracy, the Spanish court called for the extradition of several former Guatemalan government officials on charges of genocide and torture.

Anthropologist David Stoll, in his 1999 book, *Rigoberta Menchú and the Story of All Poor Guatemalans*, uncovered evidence that Menchú had changed some of the facts in her autobiography to help the guerrilla cause. He admitted, however, that the 1983 book of interviews was not a hoax and that she had only elaborated on the truth, not invented it. Menchú eventually admitted to making the changes to her story, but the Nobel committee refused to revoke the Peace Prize, citing the award was not based "primarily on the autobiography" but her life's work.

On February 12, 2007, Menchú formed the indigenous political party *Encuentro por Guatemala*. She ran for president that September as her party's candidate but received only 3 percent of the vote. Today, she is a United Nations Educational, Scientific, and Cultural Organization (UNESCO) goodwill ambassador and lives in Guatemala with her husband and children.

Crossing Borders
Summary and Analysis

In *Crossing Borders*, Guatemalan activist Rigoberta Menchú picks up the story of her life from 1981, when she goes into exile in Mexico, to 1995, when she returns to her home village of Laj Chimel. Although her early years in Guatemala are covered in the book *I, Rigoberta Menchú*, she also looks back on some of these earlier events in her life in *Crossing Borders*.

This autobiography is not told in strict chronological order but moves back and forth in time. It opens with Menchú receiving the news that she has won the 1992 Nobel Peace Prize for her efforts for human rights in her native land and elsewhere. While many of her own people in Guatemala greet the news with enthusiasm, others, especially members of the government, are skeptical and reluctant to believe it, refusing to accept or acknowledge that a full-blooded Indian could win such a great honor.

Menchú's narrative then shifts to 1995, describing her new life in Guatemala City, the nation's capital. She describes the happy anticipation of the wedding of her niece Regina Menchú Tomes, the daughter of her brother Victor, who was murdered by government agents in 1983. The occasion is marred, however, when the son of another niece, Cristina, is kidnapped. In a surprising twist, Cristina and her husband turn out to be part of the kidnapping plot, which may have been arranged primarily to embarrass Menchú.

Menchú next reflects on two contrasting homecomings, one in 1988 and the other 1994. In her initial return to Guatemala, she is treated as a notorious rebel, charged with numerous crimes against the state and has difficulty finding a lawyer to defend her in court. In 1994, by then a world celebrity and Nobel Prize winner, she received a much warmer reception.

In the book's third section, Menchú travels to the United States in 1995 for a lecture tour. While there, she receives news of a massacre in the village of Xaman, near her home. The tragedy took place during preparations for a village festival, when government soldiers arrived, argued with villagers, and then opened fire on them. Eleven people were killed and 26 injured. Going to Xaman to attend a festival, Menchú is impressed by the defiant spirit of the villagers who conduct baptisms of babies in front of the coffins of those killed in the massacre. Some of the soldiers responsible are prosecuted, but others are protected by the corrupt government.

In the book's fourth section, Menchú reflects on the trouble experienced in her own village before she left it in 1979 at age 20 with her brother and sisters. Her mother stays behind and is later tortured and killed. In Mexico, Menchú meets other exiles and Mayans who share her desire to spread word of the injustices in Guatemala. She is reunited with two of her sisters who eventually go to El Quiche in Guatemala to join the guerrilla movement in fighting the government. Menchú, however, travels to Nicaragua and later returns to Mexico to live permanently. She works tirelessly for the Committee for Peasant Unity (CUC) along with other exiles. In 1982, she travels to the United Nations in New York City to represent the CUC and becomes a member of the human rights organization the Unitary Representation of the Guatemalan Opposition (RUOG). To her dismay, Menchú finds that many UN administrators are not all that interested in her country's plight or human rights in general. She persists in her work, however, feeling that the UN, for all its flaws, is still the best platform from which to fight against the enemy.

During this time, Menchú begins to see that the struggle for indigenous peoples exists not just in Central America but around the world. In the early 1980s, she joins other advocates to form the Working Group, an organization to represent the interests of native people internationally.

In 1989, Menchú and other human rights advocates respond to the upcoming quincentenary of the Spanish "discovery" of the Americas by forming their own group to campaign for "500 Years of Resistance." They hold a continental Quincentenary Conference in Colombia to show support for the landless peasants of Brazil. Two more conferences are held in Guatemala in 1991 and Nicaragua in

1992. They lead Menchú to conclude that "It takes a lot longer [than 500 years] to destroy an ancient culture [the Maya]."

In 1995, Menchú returns to Laj Chimel, her family's village. She is shocked to see the changes. With most of the villagers either killed or driven away, outsiders have taken over much of the land with falsified deeds. Menchú lends her support to those remaining villagers, numbering only 20 families. She lives among them and helps to create a cooperative, called Tikh'al Utziil, which means "saving peace" in English.

Despite the violence and tragedy that have marked her life and those of her loved ones, Menchú remains optimistic about the future. She sees the world as "a beautiful multi-colored garden that people must accept as it is." For her, "all the ancient cultures of the Americas, are deeply embedded in every community, every village, every child, every corner."

Major Themes

Crossing Borders is an apt title for this autobiography, for Rigoberta Menchú crosses many geographic borders in her life, as she flees from and returns several times to her troubled native land. In a larger sense, she also crosses figurative borders as she comes to the realization that artificial borders cannot separate her as a Guatemalan from indigenous peoples living in other countries and continents. As she grows and matures, Menchú comes to understand that the struggle of native peoples against oppression is not an isolated but a worldwide force. She also comes to see understanding and nonviolence as the path to peace, both in Guatemala and around the world. Other major themes in this book include the evils of prejudice, the importance of heritage being passed down from one generation to another, and the never-ending struggle against injustice.

A Nation Torn Apart

The background to Menchú's life and the struggle of her people is not fully explained in *Crossing Borders,* but its effects are felt throughout the book. Guatemala enjoyed one of the most liberal dictatorships in Central America from its independence in 1821 to the 1940s. In 1944, Jorge Ubico was forced out of power, replaced by a decade of reform. Until then, *pelones,* indigenous people of Indian ancestry (primarily Mayan), were treated as second-class citizens, lived mostly in poverty, and had little say in how the country was run. *Ladinos,* Guatemalans of European stock or mixed European and Indian stock, were the ruling elite, controlling the seat of government and running most of the businesses.

A new constitution, adopted in 1945, provided all Guatemalans with certain rights, including the right to an education and to own land. Under the new government led by Colonel Jacobo Árbenz Guzmán, land reform became a major issue. Among the landowners whose parcels were seized by the government and given to peasants, was the United Fruit Company, the country's largest landowner, owned by American businessmen. The United States supported rebels rising up against the government by supplying them with money and weapons. In 1954, Guzman was overthrown, and a series of military dictatorships took over that protected the interests of the United Fruit Company. The country was not stabilized until 1963, when the army stepped in and assumed power. Leftist extremists continue to fight using guerilla tactics against the right-wing government. They looked for support in the countryside from the pelones, who often helped them in their common struggle against repression. Government troops and paramilitary organizations mercilessly attacked many villages, including Menchú's, in the 1970s and 1980s, killing and torturing anyone suspected of aiding the guerrillas. Menchú's village and many of her family members and neighbors were victims of this policy of terror. Only in the 1990s was democratic rule brought to this troubled land and some, but far from all, of the government officials responsible brought to justice.

The Mayan Spirit

Rigoberta Menchú represents the resiliency of her people, whose civilization goes back at least a thousand years in Guatemala. The ancient Maya, along with the Incas and the Aztecs, were one of the native groups that dominated Latin America in the precolonial period. Although defeated and subjugated by the Spanish invaders of the continent, the Maya continued to live in the countryside and keep their culture and traditions alive. Menchú, who calls herself a "granddaughter of the Mayan," believes the Mayan spirit kept her and her people alive and hopeful during the many years of persecution they suffered. Although spending many years in exile, Menchú continued to take pride in the heritage and folkways of her ancestors. While she identifies with her father's deep Catholic faith and visits the pope in Rome at one point, she is also proud of her mother's equally strong faith in the Mayan gods and spirits. "Mayan faith is believing in the greatness of life," she writes. This faith is clearly seen in her greatly altered native village of Laj Chimel, which she returns to several times. Although many of the villagers are killed and taken away, the survivors return to claim their land and even build a hut for Menchú when she comes to live among them for a time. Without their pride and faith in their ancestors, it is uncertain if the indigenous people of Guatemala could have survived the three decades of civil war that tore their country apart.

SHERMAN ALEXIE

Biography

SHERMAN ALEXIE represents a new generation of Native American writers who came of age in the 1980s. He was born on October 7, 1966, in Spokane, Washington, and grew up on the Spokane Indian Reservation in Willpinit, Washington. Alexie is of Spokane and Coeur d'Alene heritage. From birth, his life was filled with struggle. He was born hydrocephalic, a condition also referred to as water on the brain. At six months of age, Alexie underwent brain surgery to correct the problem. Although the surgery was successful, the doctors expected the procedure to cause him to be mentally impaired. Instead, he showed no lasting effects and was reading by the age of three.

Chronic seizures from his condition, coupled with his high intelligence, made him an outsider at the reservation school, so his parents moved him to the public high school in the town of Reardon, 20 miles away. There, he excelled in academics and sports and was a star varsity basketball player. After graduating in 1985, Alexie attended Gonzaga University in Spokane on a scholarship but withdrew after two years. He then attended Washington State University in Pullman, where he changed his major from premedical to American studies. After refusing to finish a course called Indians in American History, he left WSU in 1990. He returned four years later to graduate, the first of his tribe to earn a college degree. By then, he had already published several books, including the poetry collections *The Business of Fancydancing* and *I Would Steal Horses* and the short story collection *The Lone Ranger and Tonto Fistfight in Heaven* (1993), which earned him a PEN/Hemingway Award for best first book of fiction. His first novel, *Reservation Blues* (1995), won the Before Columbus Foundation's American Book Award and the Murray Morgan Prize. It was followed the next year by *Indian Killer* (1996), a mystery/suspense tale of a young Indian who kills white people. Alexie adapted a story from his first collection for the film *Smoke Signals* (1998) and wrote and directed the film *The Business of Fancydancing* (2002). In April 1999, Alexie made his debut as a standup comic during the Northwest Comedy Festival in Seattle. A prolific author, as of 2008, he had published 17 books including ten volumes of poetry, two additional story collections, and a young adult novel, *The Absolutely True Diary of a Part-Time Indian* (2007), which received a National Book Award for young people's literature. Since 1992, Alexie has been married to Native American Diane Tomhave. They have two sons, born in 1997 and 2001.

Sherman Alexie's work casts a harsh light on the grim realities of reservation life, but his authorial vision is softened by a wild sense of humor and a connection to the spiritual and cultural heritage of his people. There is a strong strain of social consciousness and political advocacy running through his work. His irreverent humor, contemporary characters, and direct style are in marked contrast to many of the other writers working in the Native American tradition, although his themes are not unlike those of his older contemporaries.

The Lone Ranger and Tonto Fistfight in Heaven
Summary and Analysis

This first collection of stories published by Alexie revolves around life on the Spokane Indian Reservation. The stories are semiautobiographical in nature and center on the character of Victor, an Indian youth, and his friends and family on the reservation. The stories range from first-person narratives to brief vignettes and character studies. Over the course of the book, Victor grows from adolescence to young adulthood.

In "Every Little Hurricane," the opening story, and one of the best in the collection, a very young Victor is awakened on New Year's Eve by a "hurricane," the sounds of chaos created by the drunken adults downstairs. Two of his uncles beat each other mercilessly over a trivial disagreement. The disruption caused by the intoxication and senseless violence of Victor's family members affects the impressionable boy, whose life is upended by this "hurricane." At the story's end, Victor is once again asleep between his two drunken parents. "Victor put one hand on his mother's stomach and placed the other on his father's," writes Alexie. "There was enough hunger in both, enough movement, enough geography and history, enough of everything to destroy the reservation and leave only random debris and broken furniture."

As Victor grows up, he models his own behavior after his parents' and relatives' and is caught in the destructive cycle of alcohol and drugs that define the alienation and immobility of contemporary reservation life for many. In "The Only Traffic Signal on the Reservation Doesn't Flash Red Anymore," Victor and his friend Adrian talk about Julius Windmaker, "the latest in a long line of reservation basketball heroes." A year later, Julius, once the standout athlete at the reservation school, is a drunken wreck. He plays a pickup game of basketball with Victor and Adrian and then passes out at Victor's house. The two friends turn their attention to the next up-and-coming basketball wonder, a third-grade girl named Lucy. She represents hope but also the continuation of the same cycle of thwarted aspirations. Athleticism and talent are no guarantee of escape from the misery of reservation life.

One of Victor's most compelling friends is Thomas Builds-the-Fire, who is a repository of his people's stories and past glories. However, while in the past the storyteller was an honored figure in the tribal community, Thomas is rejected by everyone on the reservation, perhaps because he reminds them of a glorious past that is too painful to contemplate. In "This Is What It Means to Say Phoenix, Arizona," Victor's father, who was introduced previously in the story "Because My Father Always Said He Was the Only Indian Who Saw Jimi Hendrix Playing 'The Star-Spangled Banner' at Woodstock," has died of a heart attack in Phoenix. A 1960s Vietnam War protester, his father had long ago become an alcoholic before abandoning his family and dying alone. Now Victor wants to claim his father's body and bring it home for tribal burial. Thomas, who Victor rejected earlier, is the only person who can help him. Thomas offers to pay for the tickets for him and Victor to fly to Phoenix, which they do and return to the reservation driving the father's pickup truck. Victor now feels ashamed for having given up on Thomas's friendship and, as the story ends, he agrees to listen to one of Thomas's imaginative stories. The ending is hopeful, as Daniel Grassian points out in his book-length study of Alexie's work. " . . . Alexie does not believe that community on the reservation or traditional Indian culture has disintegrated beyond repair," he writes. Alexie later adapted the story into the film *Smoke Signals* (1998), one of the first major Hollywood movies to be written, directed, and produced by Native Americans. The film won the Audience Award at the Sundance Film Festival.

Thomas meets his fate in the remarkable and surreal story "The Trial of Thomas Builds-the-Fire." In his trial, which suggests the darkly paranoid writing of Franz Kafka, Thomas is accused by a man from the Bureau of Indian Affairs of "a storytelling fetish accompanied by an extreme need to tell the truth." While the charges against him are never made clear, Thomas confesses to killing white soldiers in a nineteenth-century battle. His fiery speeches incite the other Indians in the courtroom and, in the end, he is sentenced to two life terms in Walla Walla Prison for his "crimes." Not even prison can silence Thomas, though. He continues to tell his stories to the other prisoners, many of them Native Americans. Thomas calls the prison "a new kind of reservation."

Major Themes

Alexie writes realistically and unsparingly of the miseries and degradation of reservation life; but he also writes of its laughter and joys. Desperation and despair are alleviated by the humor of Victor and his friends and the powerful imaginative flights of Thomas-Builds-the-Fire. These characters reappear in stories in other collections set on the Spokane Reservation. "Every theme, every story, every tragedy that exists in literature takes place in my little community," Alexie has written. " . . . It's a powerful place. I'm never going to run out of stories."

Despair of Reservation Life

Poorly educated and with no job prospects, the young people of the reservation seemingly have little to look forward to in Alexie's stories. They spend their days in idleness, drinking, and carousing. Sometimes they maliciously prey on one another, as in the story "Amusements," where Victor and his friend Sadie put the drunk and semiconscious Crazy Joe on a roller coaster just for the fun of it. At other times, Alexie's characters search for a community that no longer exists for them. In "A Drug Called Tradition," Victor, Thomas, and Junior go to a lake to take a new drug. Victor anticipates that the drug will help reconnect them with their native heritage, but it does nothing of the sort. At the end of the story, Thomas throws away what is left of the drug and Big Mom, the reservation's matriarchal figure, gives Thomas a small drum, a symbol of the traditional culture he longs for. Small as it is, the drum is a meaningful totem, far more powerful than the drug.

The Redemptive Power of the Imagination

The only hope Alexie sees for the residents of the reservation lies in the power of the imagination. "Survival = Anger x Imagination," he writes in the story "Imagining the Reservation." For him, "[i]magination is the only weapon on the reservation."

The one who wields this weapon most skillfully is Thomas Builds-the-Fire. He re-creates his people's proud past with his stories but ultimately pays a high price for it when he is sent to prison. Another character who finds refuge in his imagination is Jimmy Many Horses, who learns he is dying in "The Approximate Size of My Favorite Tumor." He fights the disease with good humor and courage. His eccentric behavior drives his wife, Norma, away, but later she returns to aid him in his final days and to make him his favorite food—fry bread, a symbol of their people's enduring and unbroken traditions. The author seems to be saying that as long as Indians use their imagination and remember the rich heritage they are the heirs to, there is hope for the future.

Indian Killer
Summary and Analysis

Indian Killer is a curious blend of suspense, murder mystery, and contemporary social drama. The novel recounts the tragic story of John Smith, a young Indian who is alienated from both his native Indian culture and the world of white society that he finds himself an unwilling part of.

John is the child of a 14-year-old Indian mother and is adopted by a middle-class white couple, Daniel and Olivia Smith. While the Smiths love John, they have little understanding of his needs. While they expose him to Indian culture, they do so more out of obligation than any sincere effort to help John understand and connect with his heritage. John never knows the tribe that he belongs to, and his lack of contact with other Indians leads him to romanticize the reservation and the people living on it. Mentally unstable, he moves further and further away from reality. The only adult he truly connects with is Father Duncan, a Spokane Indian Jesuit priest. Father Duncan teaches John to hate whites for what they have done to Indians. Although the priest mysteriously disappears when John is still a child, Father Duncan's influence is felt throughout the book, and John never forgets him.

Most of the novel takes place when John is 27 and living on his own in Seattle, Washington. A habitual loner, John has cut off all contact with his adoptive parents and labors on a construction crew building a skyscraper, because he had heard that it is a job at which Indians succeed or excel. John has no friends, and his anger and alienation lead him to develop an overwhelming desire to kill a white man. When he is insulted on the street by a young white man, he follows him. Alexie does not show John actually killing the man, and it is never completely certain that John is the "Indian Killer" of the title. The man's body is found scalped, and this sets off a hysterical manhunt in the city for the Indian Killer, a search that raises fears and simmering hatred among both white and Indian characters in the novel.

The one gleam of light in John's solitary life is his friendship with Marie Polatkin, a Native American student at the University of Washington and radical leader of the Native American Students Alliance. Marie has her own issues and problems with white society. She takes a course in Native American literature with Dr. Clarence Mather, a smug academic who is a self-appointed "expert" on Indian culture. Marie clashes with Mather over some of the required reading for the course, books that she claims were not written by real Native Americans. Marie's cousin Reggie also detests Mather, who at one point was his mentor. Their differences finally led Reggie to physically attack Mather, which resulted in Reggie's expulsion from the university. Bitter and angry, Reggie now leads a group of friends in white bashing.

David Rogers, a white student and friend of Marie's, visits an Indian-owned casino and wins a jackpot. On returning to his car in the parking lot, Rogers is killed, presumably by John Smith. Smith's next victim is a small white boy, Mark Jones, who he abducts from his upper-class home. John is touched by the boy's innocence and trusting nature, however, and does not harm him. He later returns the boy safely home, but his rage bubbles over later when he, or possibly someone else, attacks a middle-aged white businessman, Edward Letterman, as he leaves a pornography shop. Despite the man's pleas for mercy, the Indian Killer brutally kills him, tearing out his heart and eating it.

Alexie adds complexity and multiple perspectives to his narrative when he shifts the narrative to a group of young white vigilantes, led by David Rogers's brother Aaron, who prey on Indian street people and derelicts. The fires of racism against Native Americans are further fueled by Truck Schultz, a hate-mongering local radio talk-show host, who himself is nearly murdered by a shadowy figure we presume is John Smith.

Meanwhile, John's adoptive parents desperately search for him. Olivia Smith arrives at John's apartment, where she meets Jack Wilson, a local ex-cop turned successful mystery writer, who is also on John's trail. Wilson suspects John is the Indian Killer and is writing a book about him. Wilson, like Dr. Mather, is a white man who exploits Native American culture for his own ends. He claims to be part Indian himself, which helps him obtain information from Indians for his writing. Though coming from two different worlds, Jack and John share a similar background and common traits and qualities. They are both orphans searching for an identity. Both have romanticized Indian life and culture to the point that they become delusional dreamers.

In the novel's gripping climax, John kidnaps Wilson and ties him up in the unfinished skyscraper where he was previously employed. John decides not to kill Wilson but scars his face as a mark of his betrayal of Native American culture. Then, with nothing left to live for, John leaps to his death from atop the skyscraper.

The public believes the Indian Killer is finally dead, but Marie insists to the authorities that John was not the killer. She is at least partly correct. It is determined that David Rogers was not killed by John but a gang of white youths, who murdered him for his casino winnings. Wilson publishes his book about the Indian Killer, who he is convinced was John Smith. Clarence Mather writes his own book, also capitalizing on the killings. Aaron Rogers is given a light sentence for his near killing of several Indians on the street, illustrating that justice for whites and Native Americans is not always or necessarily equal. This disturbing novel ends with a Native American, possibly the Indian Killer, performing his people's traditional ghost dance. This age-old dance was meant to drive away the white presence and return Indian life to its glories in precolonial days. As the Indian Killer dances, he is joined by hundreds of other Indians. He urges the others to stand up and fight the dominant white society that for so long has suppressed them. In an ominous detail, the trees surrounding the dancers are described as "heavy with owls." Alexie is possibly subtly suggesting that evil and retribution will continue.

Major Themes

Indian Killer is Alexie's second novel and his most controversial one. More plot driven than many of his earlier short fiction, it focuses sharply on racism and the violence that it leads to. While many of the protagonists of Alexie's stories are self-destructive, in *Indian Killer*, most of the violence is directed to those seen as the enemy, whether they are white or Indian. Daniel Grassian has called the novel "an uncompromising look at rage, anger, and the violence both in the Indian community and in the larger world." Prominent themes in the books include the cathartic power of violence, the destructive power of racism and prejudice, and the appropriation of Native American culture by whites.

Alienation

Alienation runs through the book like a dark shadow, personified most fully in the central character, John Smith. Smith, whose very name evokes anonymity, is alienated from his white adoptive parents who attempt to love him, his co-workers on the construction site, and nearly everyone else he comes in contact with. As he unleashes his murderous rage against whites, the Indian Killer (perhaps Smith, Alexie teasingly never makes it clear) becomes a hunted criminal, completing his alienation from society. John's one moment of grace, other than his meetings with Marie—who cannot save him from pursuing his destructive path—is when he abducts the white boy and comes to feel true empathy for him. The possibility of change is short lived, however. Shortly after sparing the boy and returning him to his family, John again kills. Incapable of feeling anything but rage and unable to bear his alienation any longer, John chooses death. His act of self-destruction aptly takes place in the cold, uncompleted building he once helped build, a symbol of the sterile, urban world that surrounded him in life.

Alienation envelops other characters in the novel, especially Marie and her cousin who are thwarted in their desire for knowledge and an education by Dr. Mather and his control of their culture. Alienation also infects the life of Jack Wilson, an outsider who is never fully accepted by the Native Americans with which he surrounds himself. Wilson is as curiously sympathetic in his own way as John Smith is.

Racism and Violence

In *Indian Killer*, violence begets violence, and few characters are not trapped in this hopeless cycle. The murder of David Rogers, ironically committed by other white men, spurs his brother to seek vengeance on harmless Indians living in the street. Reggie's expulsion, brought about by Dr. Mather, breeds a hatred of whites that leads him to embark on a spree of white bashing with his gang. Truck Schultz uses the public airwaves to spew his unique brand of hatred and incite others to violence against Indians. Even Marie, one of the few sympathetic characters in the novel, is filled with hatred. Yet she alone feels sympathy for John Smith and sees the good in him. Part of the novel's tragedy lies in her inability to save John from his own destructive and life-destroying impulses.

Misuse and Misappropriation of Native Culture by Whites

White society dominates if not overwhelms Indians in the novel. John Smith is cut off from his roots when he is adopted by a well-intentioned but misguided white couple. Professor Mather represents an aspect of white academia that appropriates native culture and distorts and twists it to its own needs and purposes. Reggie Polatkin and his cousin Marie see through Mathers's manipulations, but they are powerless to stand up to him. Reggie's brilliant career at the college ends with his expulsion, and he turns to violence out of bitterness instead.

Jack Wilson, although a more sympathetic character than Mather, is shown to be a sham, a white man trying to pass among Indians. Wilson is even willing to turn Smith's life story into one of his books, gaining fame and money at the price of Smith's misery. The issue of what determines real Indian identity in the contemporary United States is one that is taken seriously by many Native Americans. Alexie may have been thinking of the late Native American writer Michael Dorris when he created Wilson. Dorris, who started the first program in Native American studies at Dartmouth College, asserted that he was of native heritage, but his claim was never documented by tribal records.

CHRONOLOGY

1931

- Carter Curtis Revard born on March 25 at the Osage Indian Agency town in Pawhuska, Oklahoma.

1932

- *Black Elk Speaks,* as told to John G. Neihardt, published.

1933

- *Coyote Stories* by Mourning Dove published.

1934

- N. Scott Momaday born on February 27 on the Kiowa Reservation in Lawton, Oklahoma, to Al and Natachee Momaday.
- The Wheeler-Harding Indian Reorganization Act halts further loss of reservation lands by Native Americans.
- John Joseph Matthews's only novel, *Sundown,* published.
- Gerald Vizenor born on October 22 in Minneapolis, Minnesota.

1935

- John Milton Oskison's novel *Brothers Three* appears.

1940

- James Welch is born on November 18 in Browning, Montana.

1941–45

- Approximately 2,500 Native Americans serve in the United States military during World War II.

1944

- Indian leaders found the National Congress of American Indians.

1945

- Michael Dorris born on January 30, in Louisville, Kentucky.
- Ira Hayes, a Pima Indian, helps raise the American flag at the Battle of Iwo Jima, a Japanese-held island during World War II.

1948

- Leslie Marmon Silko born on March 5, in Albuquerque, New Mexico.

1949

- D'Arcy McNickle's *They Came Here First: The Epic of the American Indian* published.
- Jay Silverheels, a Mohawk, becomes a television star playing Tonto on the popular Western series *The Long Ranger.*

1951

- Joy Harjo born on May 9 in Tulsa, Oklahoma, to Allen W. and Wynema Baker Foster.

1953

- Congress passes a resolution calling for the end of federal support and protection of some reservation Indians.

1954

- Louise Erdrich born on June 7, in Little Falls, Minnesota, to Ralph and Rita Erdrich.

1958

- *Dead Letters Sent, and Other Poems* by Maurice Kenny published.

1959

- Rigoberta Menchú born on January 9 in Laj Chimel, Quiche, Guatemala, to Vicente Menchú Perez and Juana Tum K'otoja.

1962

- Gerald Vizenor's first poetry collection, *Two Wings the Butterfly: Haiku Poems in English,* appears.

1964

- Vizenor's *Raising the Moon Vines: Original Haiku in English* published.

1965

- *Owl in the Cedar Tree*, a novel by Momaday's mother, Natachee Scott Momaday, is published.

1966

- Sherman Alexie born on October 7 in Spokane, Washington.

1967

- Momaday publishes *The Journey of Tai-me,* an early draft of *The Way to Rainy Mountain.*
- Vizenor's fourth book of haiku, *Empty Swings,* appears.

1968

- The American Indian Movement (AIM) is founded by Dennis Banks, Russell Means, and other Native American activists in Minneapolis, Minnesota.

1969

- Momaday's first novel, *House Made of Dawn,* wins the Pulitzer Prize for Fiction, and his multigenre work *The Way to Rainy Mountain* appears.

1970

- Chief Dan George is nominated for an Academy Award for best supporting actor for his performance in the film *Little Big Man.*

1972

- Dorris founds the Native American studies department at Dartmouth College in New Hampshire.
- AIM and other Indian groups occupy the headquarters of the Bureau of Indian Affairs (BIA) in Washington, D.C., to protest its policies.

1973

- AIM members seize Wounded Knee, South Dakota, to call national attention to Native American problems.

1974

- Silko's first book, *Laguna Woman,* a collection of poems, published.
- Momaday's *Angle of Geese and Other Poems* appears.
- James Welch publishes his first novel, *Winter in the Blood.*
- Simon Ortiz publishes *Going for the Rain: Poems.*

1975

- Joy Harjo's first poetry collection, *The Last Song,* published.

1976

• Momaday's *The Names: A Memoir* appears.

1977

• Silko publishes her first novel, *Ceremony*.

1978

• Simon Ortiz publishes *Howbah Indians: Stories*.
• Vizenor's science-fiction novel *Darkness in Saint Louis Bearheart* published.

1979

• Harjo's *What Moon Drove Me to This?*, a collection of poetry, published.
• Welch's second novel, *The Death of Jim Loney*, appears.

1980

• Revard publishes his first collection of poetry, *Ponca War Dances*.

1981

• Silko's multigenre work, *Storyteller*, published.
• Michael Dorris and Louise Erdrich marry.
• Wendy Rose's poetry collection *Lost Copper* is nominated for the American Book Award.

1982

• *My Name Is Rigoberta Menchú*, written by Elizabeth Burgos and based on interviews with Menchú, published.
• The film *Harold of Orange*, with a screenplay by Vizenor, is released.

1983

• Harjo's *She Had Some Horses*, a collection of poetry, published.
• Erdrich's short story "The World's Greatest Fisherman" wins the first Nelson Algren Award.
• The Olympic gold medals won by Native American athlete Jim Thorpe, taken from him because he was not strictly an amateur when he won them in 1912, are restored, thirty years after his death.

1984

• Erdrich publishes her first novel, *Love Medicine*, which is given the National Book Critics' Circle Award.

1985

• Wilma Mankiller becomes the first female chief of the Cherokee Nation.

1986

- Welch's historical novel *Fools Crow* appears.
- Erdrich's second novel, *The Beet Queen,* published.
- Anna Lee Walters's *The Sun Is Not Merciful: Short Stories* wins the American Book Award.

1987

- Dorris publishes his first novel, *A Yellow Raft in Blue Water.*
- Vizenor's novel *Griever: An American Monkey King in China* published.

1988

- Erdrich's novel *Tracks* published.

1989

- Dorris's memoir *The Broken Cord* appears.
- Momaday's *The Ancient Child* published.
- Erdrich's *Baptism of Desire,* a collection of poems, published.
- Harjo's *Secrets from the Center of the World* appears.

1990

- Joy Harjo's poetry collection *In Mad Love and War* receives the American Book Award.
- Welch's novel *The Indian Lawyer* published.
- Elizabeth Cook-Lyman publishes *The Power of Horses and Other Stories.*
- Gerald Vizenor's *Bearheart: Heirship Chronicles*, a rewriting of *Darkness in Saint Louis Bearheart,* appears.

1991

- The novel *The Crown of Columbus,* the only acknowledged collaboration of Dorris and Erdrich, appears.
- Silko's second novel, *Almanac of the Dead,* published.
- Momaday's *In the Presence of the Sun: A Gathering of Shields* published.
- *Lakota Woman,* a biography by Mary Brave Bird, wins the American Book Award.
- Vizenor's *Landfill Meditations: Crossblood Stories* appears.

1992

- Menchú is awarded the Nobel Peace Prize.
- Alexie's first book, *The Business of Fancydancing,* a collection of poems, published.
- Revard's poetry collection *Cowboys and Indians Christmas Shopping* appears.
- Ben Nighthorse Campbell is elected U.S. Senator from Colorado. He is the third Native American to serve in the Senate.

1993

- Alexie's first collection of short stories, *The Lone Ranger and Tonto Fistfight in Heaven,* is awarded a PEN/Hemingway Award for best first book of fiction.
- Erdrich's revised and expanded version of *Love Medicine* published.
- Silko's *Sacred Water*, a collection of photographs and essays, published.
- Wilma Mankiller's autobiography, *A Chief and Her People*, appears.

1994

- Momaday's *Circle of Wonder: A Native American Christmas Story* published.
- Erdrich's novel *The Bingo Palace* published.
- Harjo's *The Woman Who Fell From the Sky,* a book of poems, appears.
- Greg Sarris publishes *Grand Avenue,* a short story collection.
- Susan Power's novel *The Grass Dancer* published.

1995

- Alexie publishes his first novel, *Reservation Blues.*
- Erdrich's memoir *The Blue Jay's Dance: A Birth Year* published.

1996

- Alexie's second novel, *Indian Killer,* wins the American Book Award.
- Silko's *Yellow Woman and a Beauty of the Spirit: Essays on Native American Life Today* published.
- Erdrich's novel *Tales of Burning Love* and her children's story *Grandmother's Pigeon* published.

1997

- Revard's poetry collection *An Eagle Nation* appears.
- Dorris commits suicide at age 52 on April 10 in Concord, New Hampshire.
- Momaday's *The Man Made of Words: Essays, Stories, Passages* published.
- Maria Tallchief's autobiography, *Maria Tallchief: America's Prima Ballerina,* appears.
- *Native American Literature: A Brief Introduction and Anthology*, edited by Vizenor, published.

1998

- Menchú's autobiography *Crossing Borders* appears, and she is awarded the Prince of Asturias Award.
- Erdrich's *The Antelope Wife* published.
- *Smoke Signals*, a film with screenplay by Alexie based on his short story, released.

1999

- Momaday's *In The Bear's House* published.
- Revard's memoir and essays *Family Matters, Tribal Affairs* appears.

2000

- Harjo publishes the children's book *The Good Luck Cat.*
- Alexie's *One Stick Song* and *The Toughest Indian in the World* published.
- Welch's last novel, *The Heartsong of Charging Elk,* appears.
- Vizenor's *Chancers* published.

2001

- Revard's *Winning the Dust Bowl* published.

2002

- Harjo's *How We Became Human: New and Selected Poems 1975–2001* published.
- The film *The Business of Fancydancing,* written and directed by Alexie, released.

2003

- Erdrich publishes *The Master Butchers Singing Club,* a mystery.
- Alexie's *Ten Little Indians* published.
- James Welch dies on August 4.

2005

- Revard's *How the Songs Come Down* published.

2006

- David Treuer publishes *The Translations of Dr. Apelles* and *Native American Fiction: A User's Manual.*
- Vizenor's poetry collection *Almost Ashore* published.

2007

- Alexie's first novel for young adults, *The Absolutely True Diary of a Part-Time Indian,* published and is honored with the National Book Award for young people's literature.
- Momaday receives the National Medal of the Arts from President George W. Bush.
- Menchú is defeated in the first round of voting in the Guatemalan presidential election.

2008

- Erdrich's *The Plague of Doves* published and is named, the following year, a finalist for the Pulitzer Prize for Fiction.

ADDITIONAL READING

Bearheart: Heirship Chronicles by Gerald Vizenor

A fascinating science-fiction novel-within-a-novel, the title character has produced a novel about a shaman's journey from Wisconsin to New Mexico during a nightmarish future. He allows a young woman to read his work during the American Indian takeover of the Bureau of Indian Affairs, where Bearheart works. The tale is filled with Indian lore and trickster magic and makes an intriguing counterpoint to the contemporary story.

Eye Killers by Aaron Carr

What may be the first vampire novel by a Native American writer, *Eye Killers* is the story of part-Navajo Melissa Roanhorse, who has been chosen as the latest bride of Falke, a vampire. Her grandfather Michael sets out to save her from her terrible fate with his Navajo traditions and magic as his only weapons against the undead. A chilling and impressive thriller.

Grand Avenue by Greg Sarris

A novel composed of ten interlinked stories, all set in the poorest neighborhood of Santa Rosa, a small city in Northern California. Each story is narrated by a different member of a doomed clan of Pimo Indians, whose lives are marked by a cycle of alcohol abuse and violence, broken intermittently by hope and humor.

The Grass Dancer by Susan Power

This ambitious and powerful first novel chronicles the often grim lives of the residents of a Sioux reservation over the course of a century. The history begins with Red Dress, a Sioux maiden who is murdered by a mentally unbalanced white preacher and loved by Ghost Something, who loses his own grip on sanity over the death. Their spirits haunt their descendants who grapple with challenges of their own.

Howbah Indians: Stories by Simon J. Ortiz

A collection of short stories that are both tragic and comic in a way characteristic of the Acoma Indians, the tribe from which the author is descended.

Little by David Treuer

The title character of this impressive first novel is a physically challenged 8-year-old of mixed heritage who is dead at the story's start. The residents of Poverty, a crumbling housing project on a reservation in northern Minnesota, tell their lives in first-person narrative and in the process reveal the life of Little, whose vocabulary was restricted to the single word *you*.

Tracks by Louise Erdrich

Edrich's third novel revisits some of the characters from *Love Medicine* at earlier points in their lives. Set in the early 1900s in North Dakota, it introduces Fleur Pillager, an Indian woman of strange powers who brings the conflict between two Chippewa families to a point of crisis.

The Way to Rainy Mountain by N. Scott Momaday

Momaday's followup book to *House Made of Dawn* is an intriguing multigenre work that skillfully interweaves historical vignettes, personal narrative, and old Kiowa stories and legends to tell about the author's journey to his homeland. Its impact is heightened by drawings created by the author's father.

BIBLIOGRAPHY

Books

Allen, Paula Gunn. *The Sacred Hoop: Recovering the Feminine in American Indian Traditions.* Boston: Beacon Press, 1986.

Arnold, Ellen L., ed. *Conversations with Leslie Marmon Silko.* Jackson: University Press of Mississippi, 2000.

Barnett, Louise K., and James L. Thorson, eds. *Leslie Marmon Silko: A Collection of Critical Essays.* Albuquerque: University of New Mexico Press, 1999.

Beidler, Peter G., and Gay Barton. *A Reader's Guide to the Novels of Louise Erdrich.* Columbia: University of Missouri Press, 1999.

Blaeser, Kim. *Gerald Vizenor: Writing in the Oral Tradition.* Norman: University of Oklahoma Press, 1996.

Bloom, Harold, ed. *Native American Writers.* Bloom's Modern Critical Views series. New York: Chelsea House, 2010.

Bruchac, Joseph, ed. *Survival This Way: Interviews with American Indian Poets.* Tucson: University of Arizona Press, 1987.

Chavkin, Allan, ed. *The Chippewa Landscape of Louise Erdrich.* Tuscaloosa: University of Alabama Press, 1999.

Coltelli, Laura, ed. *Joy Harjo: The Spiral of Memory: Interviews.* Ann Arbor: University of Michigan Press, 1996.

Fitz, Brewster E. *Silko: Writing Storyteller and Medicine Woman.* Norman: University of Oklahoma Press, 2004.

Grassian, Daniel. *Understanding Sherman Alexie.* Columbia: University of South Carolina Press, 2005.

Hobson, Geary, ed. *The Remembered Earth: An Anthology of Contemporary American Indian Literature.* Albuquerque: University of New Mexico Press, 1980.

Jaskoski, Helen. *Leslie Marmon Silko: A Study of the Short Fiction.* New York: Twayne Publishers, 1998.

Josephy, Alvin M., Jr. *Now That the Buffalo's Gone: A Study of Today's American Indians.* Norman: University of Oklahoma Press, 1984.

Katz, Jane B., ed. *This Song Remembers: Self-Portraits of Native Americans in the Arts.* Boston: Houghton Mifflin, 1980.

Keegan, Marcia. *Pueblo People: Ancient Traditions and Modern Lives.* Santa Fe, NM: Clear Light Publishers, 1999.

Larson, Charles R. *American Indian Fiction.* Albuquerque: University of New Mexico Press, 1980.

Lee, A. Robert ed. *Loosening the Seams: Interpretations of Gerald Vizenor.* Bowling Green, OH: Bowling Green State University Popular Press, 2000.

Lincoln, Kenneth. *Native American Renaissance.* Berkeley: University of California Press, 1983.

McFarland, Ronald E., ed. *James Welch.* Lewiston, ID: Confluence Press, 1986.

———. *Understanding James Welch.* Columbia: University of South Carolina Press, 2000.

Nelson, Robert M. *Place and Vision: The Function of Landscape in Native American Fiction.* New York: Peter Lang Publishing, 1993.

Ortiz, Simon. *Earth Power Coming: Short Fiction in Native American Literature.* Tsaiale, AZ: Navajo Community College Press, 1983.

Porter, Joy, and Kenneth M. Roemer, eds. *The Cambridge Companion to Native American Literature.* New York: Cambridge University Press, 2005.

Roemer, Kenneth, ed. *Approaches to Teaching Momaday's The Way to Rainy Mountain.* New York: Modern Language Association, 1988.

Salyer, Greg. *Leslie Marmon Silko.* New York: Twayne, 1997.

Scarberry-Garcia, Susan. *Landmarks of Healing: A Study of House Made of Dawn.* Albuquerque: University of New Mexico Press, 1990.

Schubnell, Matthias. *N. Scott Momaday: The Cultural and Literary Background.* Norman: University of Oklahoma Press, 1985.

Schweninger, Lee. *N. Scott Momaday* (Literary Masters series, Vol. 12). Detroit: Gale Group, 2001.

Seyersted, Per. *Leslie Marmon Silko.* Western Writers Series 45. Boise, ID: Boise State University Press, 1980.

Stookey, Lorena L. *Louise Erdrich: A Critical Companion.* Westport, Conn.: Greenwood Press, 1999.

Swann, Brian, and Arnold Krupat, eds. *Recovering the Word: Essays on Native American Literature.* Berkeley: University of California Press, 1987.

Trafzer, Clifford, ed. *Blue Dawn, Red Earth: New Native American Storytellers.* New York: Doubleday, 1996.

Trimble, Martha Scott. *N. Scott Momaday.* Western Writers Series 9. Boise, ID: Boise State University Press, 1973.

Turner, Frederick, ed. *The Portable North American Indian Reader.* New York: Viking Press, 1974.

Velie, Alan R., ed. *American Indian Literature: An Anthology.* Norman: University of Oklahoma Press, 1979.

———. *Four American Literary Masters: N. Scott Momaday, James Welch, Leslie Marmon Silko, and Gerald Vizenor.* Norman: University of Oklahoma Press, 1982.

Vizenor, Gerald. *Shadow Distance: A Gerald Vizenor Reader.* Hanover, NH: Wesleyan University Press, 1994.

Volborth, Judith Mountain Leaf. *Thunder Root: Traditional and Contemporary Native American Verse.* Los Angeles: University of California at Los Angeles American Indian Studies Center Series, 1978.

Wiget, Andrew. *Native American Literature.* Boston: Twayne Publishers, 1985.

Wild, Peter. *James Welch.* Western Writers Series 57. Boise, ID: Boise State University Press, 1983.

Wilson, Norma C. *The Nature of Native American Poetry.* Albuquerque: University of New Mexico Press, 2001.

Witherspoon, Gary. *Language and Art in the Navajo Universe.* Ann Arbor: University of Michigan Press, 1977.

Woodard, Charles L. *Ancestral Voice: Conversations with N. Scott Momaday.* Lincoln: University of Nebraska Press, 1989.

Websites

Academy of Achievement: N. Scott Momaday
http://www.achievement.org/autodoc/page/momObio-1

Homepage for Leslie Marmon Silko
http://literati.net/Silko/index.htm

James Welch Biography
http://biography.jrank.org/pages/4818/Welch-James.html

Joy Harjo's Blog
http://www.joyharjo.com/news/

Native American Authors Project: Carter Revard
http://www.ipl.org/div/natam/bios/browse.pl/A6

Native American Authors Project: Michael Dorris
http://www.ipl.org/div/natam/bios/browse.pl/A32

Native American Authors—Teacher Resources
http://falcon.jmu.edu/~remseyil/natuath.htm

Native Wiki: Gerald Vizenor
http://www.nativewiki.org/Gerald_Vizenor

Native Wiki: Joy Harjo
http://www.nativewiki.org/Joy_Harjo

Native Wiki: Michael Dorris
http://www.nativewiki.org/Michael_Dorris

Nobel Prize: Rigoberta Menchú Tum
http://nobelprize.org/nobel_prizes/peace/laureates/1992/index.html

Official Website of Sherman Alexie
http://www.fallsapart.com/

Voices from the Gaps: Louise Erdrich
http://voices.cla.umn.edu/vg/Bios/entries/erdrich_louise.html

Women's History: Louise Erdrich
http://www.gales.cengage.com/free_resources/whm/bio/erdrich_l.htm

INDEX

PICTURE CREDITS

ABOUT THE AUTHOR

STEVEN OTFINOSKI has written more than 130 books for young adults. He is the author of *Nineteenth-Century Writers* and *Great Black Writers* in Facts On File's American Profiles series. He lives in Connecticut with his wife, Beverly, a teacher and editor.